CHICAGO TRAVEL GUIDE 2023

Unforgettable Experiences in Chicago: Luxury and Budget-Friendly Attractions, Accommodations, Dining, Shopping, Nightlife and Entertainment and more

By

Eric J. Richardson

Table Of Contents

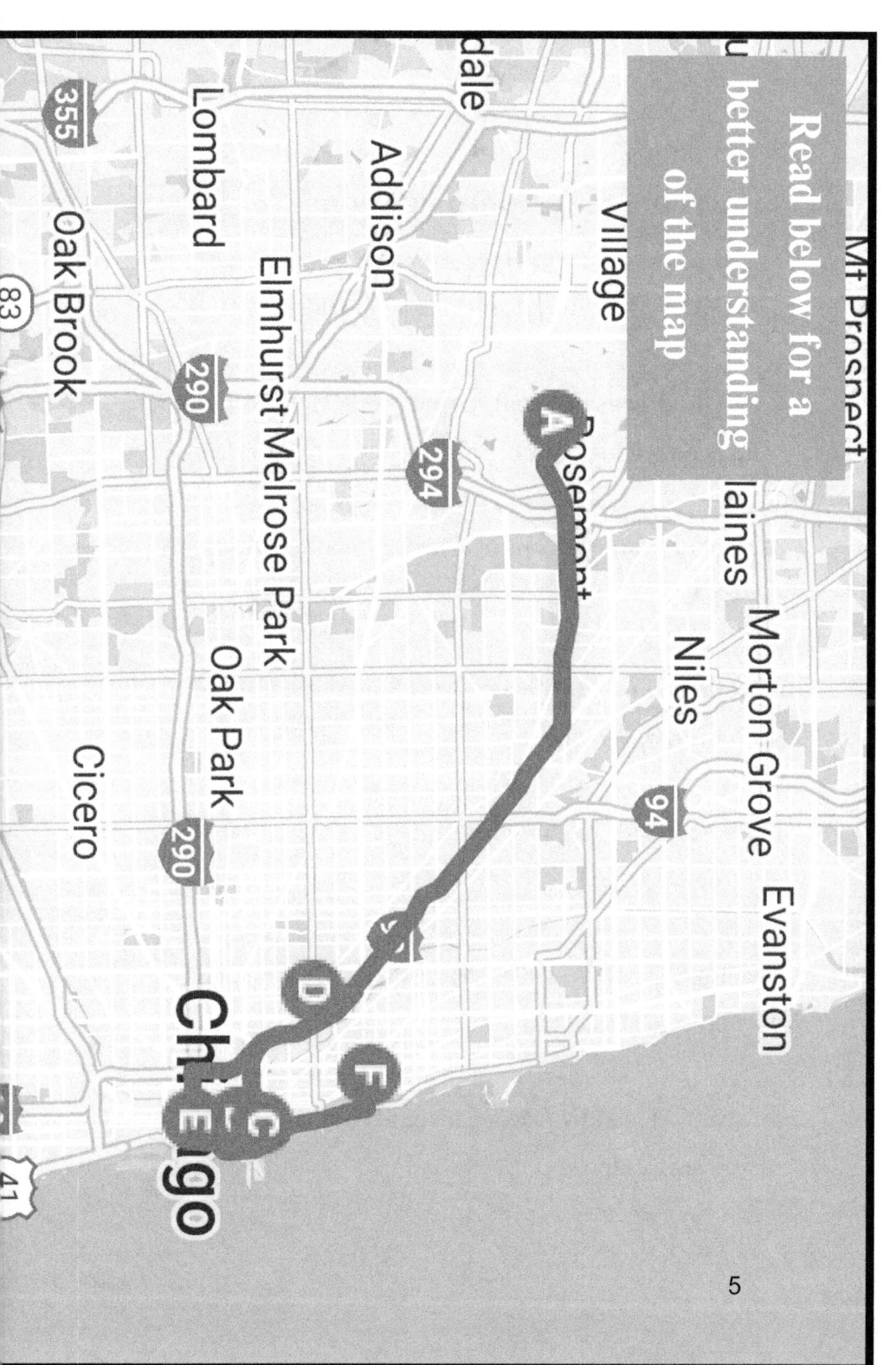

Airport to Accommodations

Directions from O'Hare Airport International (ORD), West Balmoral Avenue in Chicago, IL, USA.

A

O'Hare International Airport (ORD), West Balmoral Avenue, Chicago, IL, United States of America

B

North Wabash Avenue, The Langham, Chicago, IL, USA

C

The Peninsula Chicago, East Superior Street in Chicago, Illinois.

D

West North Avenue, Chicago, IL, United States The Robey

E

East Ida B. Wells Drive, Chicago, IL, USA, HI Chicago Hostel

F

West Arlington Place, Chicago, IL, USA, Chicago Getaway Hostel

Introduction

Welcome to Chicago, the dynamic and busy city on Lake Michigan's shoreline! This spectacular city welcomes your exploration whether you arrive by plane, rail, or vehicle. As soon as you walk into the bustling streets, you'll be attracted by the distinct energy that pervades the air.

Prepare to be immersed in a city that perfectly mixes a rich past with a contemporary metropolitan setting when you arrive. Chicago is known for its beautiful architecture, diversified neighborhoods, world-class food, and vibrant arts and culture scene. This cityscape will take your breath away with its distinctive skyline decorated with tall buildings.

As you go further into the city, you will come across a lively tapestry of neighborhoods, each with its unique personality. Every part of Chicago has something distinctive to offer, from the busy streets of Downtown, where the Magnificent Mile entices shoppers and the Loop exhibits the city's iconic architecture, to the bohemian atmosphere of Wicker Park and the pulsating energy of the South Side's Hyde Park.

The city's cultural scene reflects its dynamic character. Explore world-class institutions such as the Art Institute of Chicago, which holds a massive collection of masterpieces, or see a show at the historic Chicago Theatre. Music enthusiasts will find their groove at the cradle of blues and jazz, where they may groove to live performances in tiny bars or at famous events such as the Chicago Blues and Jazz Festival.

Chicago is a foodie's dream when it comes to gastronomic pleasures. A deep-dish pizza loaded with hot dogs, and the famed Italian beef sandwiches await your taste buds. Aside from these historic landmarks, the city has a vibrant gastronomy scene, with a diversity of different cuisines and creative dining experiences to delight even the most discriminating palates.

Throughout your visit, you'll notice that Chicagoans are famed for their friendliness and kindness. Don't be afraid to start up a discussion with a local, as they are typically happy to share their favorite sites, provide suggestions, and share their enthusiasm for the city.

Whether you're here for a few days or a few weeks, Chicago will leave an unforgettable imprint on your heart. So prepare for an incredible adventure through a city that proudly celebrates its history while always embracing the future. Hello and welcome to Chicago!

Chicago at a Glance

Fast Facts about Chicago

Chicago, located in Illinois, is a vibrant city on the southwestern shore of Lake Michigan. It is the third most populous city in the United States, known for its impressive architecture, diverse culture, and iconic culinary offerings.

Nicknamed the "Windy City," Chicago's moniker is said to be derived from its strong winds or the loquaciousness of its politicians. The city boasts a skyline adorned with architectural marvels, including the birthplace of modern skyscrapers.

With a continental climate, Chicago experiences hot summers and cold winters, often accompanied by dramatic weather changes and occasional thunderstorms.

The city's transportation system is well-developed, with the Chicago Transit Authority (CTA) operating an extensive network of buses and trains. O'Hare International Airport and Midway International Airport serve as major hubs for domestic and international travel.

Chicago is a sports enthusiast's paradise, home to teams like the Chicago Cubs (baseball), Chicago White Sox (baseball), Chicago Bulls (basketball), Chicago Bears (American football), and Chicago Blackhawks (ice hockey).

Culturally, Chicago offers a plethora of attractions, including world-class museums such as the Art Institute of Chicago and the Field Museum. The city hosts numerous festivals throughout the year, celebrating music, art, food, and more.

When it comes to cuisine, Chicago is renowned for its unique dishes. Deep-dish pizza, Chicago-style hot dogs, Italian beef sandwiches, and the city's famous Garrett Popcorn Shops' Chicago-style popcorn are beloved local specialties.

These fast facts merely scratch the surface of what Chicago has to offer. Its rich culture, architectural wonders, diverse culinary scene, and friendly atmosphere make it an enticing destination for visitors seeking an unforgettable urban experience.

Neighborhoods in Chicago

Chicago is a metropolis of varied neighborhoods, each with its distinct personality and charm. Here are some of the famous neighborhoods to visit while in the city:

The Loop: Located in the city's downtown area, the Loop is the central business district of Chicago. It is home to iconic skyscrapers, including the Willis Tower (formerly Sears Tower), as well as cultural institutions like the Art Institute of Chicago and Millennium Park.

River North: Situated just north of the Loop, River North is known for its vibrant art scene and trendy dining establishments. It houses numerous art galleries, upscale boutiques, and some of the city's best-known restaurants.

Lincoln Park: This neighborhood is named after the expansive Lincoln Park, which stretches along the lakefront. It offers a mix of residential areas, beautiful parks, and attractions such as the Lincoln Park Zoo and the Peggy Notebaert Nature Museum.

Wicker Park: Wicker Park is a vibrant neighborhood known for its bohemian atmosphere, artistic community, and trendy shops and eateries. It is a hub for music, street art, and independent boutiques.

Logan Square: Located on the Northwest Side, Logan Square has a hip and eclectic vibe. It features a lively culinary scene, diverse nightlife options, and the historic Logan Square Park.

Hyde Park: Situated on the South Side, Hyde Park is home to the prestigious University of Chicago and the renowned Museum of Science and Industry. It has a rich intellectual and cultural heritage and offers beautiful parks and historic architecture.

Pilsen: Known for its Mexican heritage and vibrant arts scene, Pilsen is a neighborhood on the Lower West Side. It is characterized by colorful murals, street art, authentic Mexican cuisine, and a strong sense of community.

Lakeview: As the name suggests, Lakeview is a neighborhood along the lakefront. It offers a lively nightlife scene, diverse dining options, and Wrigley Field, the historic home of the Chicago Cubs.

Gold Coast: Located on the Near North Side, the Gold Coast is one of Chicago's most affluent neighborhoods. It is known for its historic mansions, upscale shopping on the Magnificent Mile, and proximity to the lakefront.

South Loop: Situated just south of the downtown area, the South Loop has undergone significant development in recent years. It is home to a mix of residential buildings, cultural institutions like the Museum Campus, and Grant Park, also known as "Chicago's front yard."

These are just a few of the many vibrant neighborhoods that make up the fabric of Chicago. Each one offers a unique experience, reflecting the city's diversity, culture, and community spirit. Exploring these neighborhoods is a great way to immerse yourself in the local atmosphere and discover the true essence of Chicago.

Weather and Climate in Chicago

Chicago experiences a continental climate, characterized by distinct seasons and variable weather patterns. Here's an overview of the weather and climate in Chicago:

Summers (June to August): Summers in Chicago are generally warm and humid. Average high temperatures range from the mid-70s to the mid-80s Fahrenheit (mid-20s to low 30s Celsius). However, heatwaves can push temperatures into the 90s Fahrenheit (mid-30s Celsius) or higher. It's advisable to dress in light, breathable clothing during this season.

Autumns (September to November): Autumn brings colder temperatures and changing foliage to Chicago. Early autumn may still be moderate, with temperatures in the 60s to 70s Fahrenheit (15 to 25 degrees Celsius), although temperatures progressively drop into the forties and fifties Fahrenheit (5 to 15 degrees Celsius) later in the season. Layered clothing is advised since temperatures might change throughout the day.

Winters (December to February): Winters in Chicago can be cold and snowy. Average high temperatures range from the 30s to the low 40s Fahrenheit (around 0 to 5 degrees Celsius), while average lows dip into the 20s Fahrenheit (around -5 degrees Celsius). However, temperatures can occasionally drop well below freezing, with wind chills making it feel even colder. Heavy snowfall is common, so it's important to dress warmly with appropriate winter clothing.

Springs (March to May): Springs in Chicago are characterized by gradually warming temperatures. Early spring can still be chilly, with highs in the 40s to 50s Fahrenheit (5 to 15 degrees Celsius). As the season progresses, temperatures rise into the 60s and 70s Fahrenheit (15 to 25 degrees Celsius). Layered clothing is recommended during this transitional season.

Chicago is also known for its variable weather conditions, which can change rapidly. It's advisable to check the local weather forecast before your visit and be prepared for potential weather changes. The city experiences occasional thunderstorms, particularly during the summer months.

In addition, Chicago is often subject to strong winds due to its location near Lake Michigan. These winds can add a chill factor, especially during the colder months. It's recommended to carry a light jacket or sweater even during the summer.

Overall, Chicago's weather and climate offer distinct seasons, with each season bringing its unique charm and activities. Whether you're enjoying the sunshine of summer, the colors of autumn, the winter wonderland, or the blossoming of spring, Chicago's climate adds to the city's vibrant atmosphere.

Chapter1: Getting to and Around Chicago

Transportation Options to Chicago

Getting to Chicago offers a range of transportation options to suit your needs. Here are some detailed explanations of the different ways you can reach the city:

Air Travel:

Chicago is connected to the world by O'Hare International Airport (ORD) and Midway International Airport (MDW). O'Hare International Airport is one of the busiest in the world, with a diverse range of domestic and international flights. It's roughly 17 miles (27 kilometers) northwest of Chicago. Midway Airport is located about 10 miles (16 kilometers) southwest of downtown and mostly handles domestic aircraft. Trains, buses, and taxis are available at both airports to carry you into the city center.

Train Travel:

Union Station in downtown Chicago is the city's main train station. Amtrak provides train service to Chicago, connecting it to various cities across the United States. Amtrak offers different classes of service, including coach, business class, and sleeper accommodations. Trains provide comfortable seating, onboard amenities like Wi-Fi and power outlets, and the opportunity to enjoy scenic views during your journey.

Bus Travel:

Chicago has several bus companies operating routes to and from the city. Greyhound, Megabus, and BoltBus are popular choices that connect Chicago to numerous destinations across the United States and Canada. Buses offer comfortable seating, Wi-Fi, power outlets, and affordable fares. The bus terminals are located conveniently in downtown Chicago, making it easy to access other parts of the city upon arrival.

Car Travel:

Chicago has a well-developed road network, making it accessible by car. Major interstates that pass through or near Chicago include I-90 (Jane Addams Memorial Tollway), I-94 (Dan Ryan Expressway), and I-290 (Eisenhower Expressway). Depending on your starting location, you can plan your route using GPS navigation systems or traditional maps. Keep in mind that traffic conditions can vary, so it's advisable to check for any potential delays, especially during peak hours.

By considering these transportation options, you can select the most suitable and convenient way to get to

Chicago, based on factors such as cost, comfort, and personal preferences.

Getting to Chicago from outside the United States offers several transportation options. Here are some detailed explanations of the different ways you can reach the city:

International Flights:

The most common and convenient way to reach Chicago from outside the United States is by air travel.

O'Hare International Airport (ORD) is one of the busiest airports in the world and serves as a major international gateway to the city.

Many international airlines offer direct flights to Chicago from various countries, making it easily accessible.

Depending on your location, you can check with airlines that provide direct flights or consider connecting flights through major hubs.

Connecting Flights:
If there are no direct flights available from your location, connecting flights are a common option.
Many major international airports offer connecting flights to Chicago.
You can search for flights with layovers in cities like New York, Los Angeles, London, Frankfurt, or Dubai, among others, that have good connectivity to Chicago.
Be sure to check the layover duration to allow enough time for immigration, customs, and transfers.

Airlines and Ticket Booking:
Research and compare different airlines to find the most convenient and cost-effective options.

Visit airline websites or use online travel agencies to search for flights, compare prices, and book tickets. Consider factors like flight duration, layover duration, baggage allowance, and any additional services or amenities offered by the airlines.

Airport Transfers:
Upon arrival at O'Hare International Airport, there are various transportation options to reach downtown Chicago.
The airport provides taxi services, and ride-sharing options like Uber and Lyft, as well as public transportation such as the Blue Line train that connects directly to downtown.
Midway International Airport also offers similar transportation options to reach the city.

Customs and Immigration:
Before traveling to the United States, make sure to review the entry requirements and necessary travel

documents, such as a valid passport and appropriate visas or ESTA (Electronic System for Travel Authorization) for eligible countries participating in the Visa Waiver Program.

Upon arrival in Chicago, you will go through customs and immigration checks before proceeding to the baggage claim area.

Other Transportation Options:

If you prefer alternative modes of transportation, you can consider traveling by sea or land.

Cruise ships and ferries operate in nearby ports such as Chicago's Navy Pier, offering a unique way to arrive in the city.

Trains, buses, or rental cars can be options if you are traveling from neighboring countries or regions.

It's essential to plan your trip well in advance, considering factors like flight availability, travel restrictions, and visa requirements. Checking with airlines, travel agencies, and official government websites will provide you with the most up-to-date information on flights, entry requirements, and any travel advisories.

Tips for Finding the Best Deals on Flights

Finding the greatest offers on flights to Chicago may help you save money and make your trip more reasonable. Here are some pointers to help you discover cheap flights:

Be Flexible About Your Trip Dates: Being flexible about your trip dates might have a substantial influence on the cost of your tickets.

Consider going during off-peak seasons or on weekdays, since rates are often cheaper than on weekends or during high travel times.

Use travel websites' flexible date search features to compare rates across multiple dates and choose the most inexpensive choices.

Book Early: Booking your flights early may typically result in cheaper pricing.

Airlines typically post travel schedules and tickets around 11 months in advance, so reserving early will help you acquire cheaper costs.

To prevent losing out on discounts, keep an eye on pricing and book when you locate a decent bargain.

Subscribe to Price Alerts:

Subscribe to fare alerts or price-tracking websites to be notified when fares for flights to Chicago decrease.

You may tailor the notifications to your specific trip dates and departure airports.

When you get price drop alerts, act fast to take advantage of the lower rates.

Price Comparison on Multiple Travel Websites:

Don't stick to just one travel website. To locate the greatest bargains, compare prices across several sites.

Expedia, Kayak, Skyscanner, and Google Flights, among other popular travel websites, can give a complete overview of available flights and costs.

To compare rates, use several search engines and travel agents, since they may offer unique discounts or relationships with certain airlines.

Keep an open mind about different departure airports:

Check for flights from neighboring airports, since they may have cheaper tickets or more alternatives.

Consider looking for flights from airports in surrounding locations such as Milwaukee or Indianapolis, which are within a comfortable driving distance of Chicago.

Think about connecting flights:

Direct flights to Chicago may be more convenient, but connecting flights are often less expensive.

Compare rates for direct and connecting flights using search engines, and assess the savings against the extra travel time and any layovers.

Participate in Loyalty Programs:

Enroll in frequent flier or reward programs provided by airlines.

Earn miles or points for your trips and take advantage of special specials or discounts available only to program members.

This may result in future discounts or even free flights, allowing you to save money in the long term.

Clear Cookies in Your Browser or Use Incognito Mode:

Some travel websites may keep track of your browser history and raise rates depending on your search habits.

Clear your browser cookies or use incognito mode when looking for flights to prevent this.

This might assist you in seeing the most accurate and impartial costs.

When looking for flight discounts to Chicago, remember to be patient, attentive, and adaptable. With these techniques, you can improve your chances of finding cheap flights and make your trip experience more cost-effective.

Best Time To Visit

The best time to visit Chicago depends on various factors such as weather preferences, popular events, and budget considerations. Here's an overview of different seasons to help you determine the ideal time for your visit:

Spring (March to May):
Spring in Chicago is a transitional season with fluctuating temperatures. The city starts to come

alive with blossoming flowers and vibrant greenery. It's an excellent time to explore outdoor attractions, enjoy cultural festivals, and experience fewer crowds compared to summer. Keep in mind that occasional rain showers are common during this season. Pack layers to accommodate temperature changes.

Summer (June to August):
Summer is the peak tourist season in Chicago. Expect pleasant weather with warm temperatures. The city buzzes with activity, and popular attractions like Millennium Park, Navy Pier, and Lake Michigan beaches are bustling with visitors. Outdoor concerts, street festivals, and fireworks displays are prevalent during this time. However, hotel rates and flight prices tend to be higher, and popular attractions can get crowded, especially on weekends and holidays.

Fall (September to November):

Fall is a beautiful time to visit Chicago. The weather is generally pleasant, with mild temperatures and vibrant foliage. The city hosts various cultural events and music festivals, including the renowned Chicago International Film Festival. Hotel rates and crowds tend to decrease compared to summer, making it a favorable time for budget-conscious travelers. Pack layers to accommodate temperature fluctuations.

Winter (December to February):

Winter in Chicago can be cold, with occasional snowfall. Despite the cold weather, the city transforms into a winter wonderland with festive decorations, ice skating rinks, and holiday markets. Indoor attractions like museums, theaters, and shopping along the Magnificent Mile offer entertainment. Hotel rates are generally lower during this season, except during major events like New

Year's Eve. Be prepared for colder temperatures, snowstorms, and limited outdoor activities.

Considering these factors, the best time to visit Chicago is typically during the spring (March to May) and fall (September to November) seasons. These months offer milder weather, fewer crowds, and more affordable prices compared to the peak summer season. However, if you enjoy warm weather, vibrant festivals, and outdoor activities, then summer would be the ideal time despite the higher costs and larger crowds. Conversely, if you enjoy winter activities, and cultural events, and don't mind the cold, then winter can be a magical time to experience the city's festive atmosphere.

Transportation Options in Chicago

When it comes to navigating Chicago conveniently, you have several transportation options to choose from. Here's a detailed overview of the various means of transportation available in the city:

Chicago Transit Authority (CTA):
The CTA operates an extensive network of buses and trains that provide convenient transportation throughout Chicago and its suburbs.
The 'L' train system consists of several lines (Red, Blue, Brown, Green, Orange, Pink, Purple, and Yellow) that cover the city and major attractions.
Buses cover areas not served by the train system and provide additional connectivity.
Fares can be paid using a reloadable Ventra Card, which can be purchased at stations, or with contactless payment methods like smartphones and credit/debit cards.
The CTA offers daily, weekly, and monthly passes for unlimited rides within a specific period, providing cost-effective options for frequent travelers.

Metra:

Metra is a commuter rail system that serves the Chicago metropolitan area, connecting the city with its suburbs and neighboring states. It operates several lines, including Union Pacific, BNSF, Milwaukee District, and more. Metra is a convenient option for those commuting from the suburbs to downtown Chicago or vice versa.. Fares are based on the distance traveled, and discounted passes are available for regular commuters.

Taxis and Rideshares:

Taxis and rideshare services like Uber and Lyft are widely available in Chicago.Taxis can be hailed on the street or found at designated taxi stands. Rideshare services can be accessed through smartphone apps, allowing you to request a car for pick-up at your location.

Taxis and rideshares are convenient options for door-to-door transportation, especially if you have heavy luggage or prefer a more private travel experience. Fare rates vary based on distance and time traveled.

Divvy Bikes:

Divvy is a bike-sharing program that allows you to rent bicycles from various stations throughout the city. You can access a bike by purchasing a pass or using a credit card at the station's kiosk. Divvy bikes are a great way to explore Chicago's neighborhoods and lakefront trails at your own pace. The system provides both single-trip options and day passes for unlimited 30-minute rides within 24 hours.

Rental Cars:

Rental cars are readily available in Chicago, with several rental agencies operating throughout the city. Renting a car gives you the flexibility to explore not only the city but also nearby attractions and suburbs.

However, keep in mind that parking in downtown Chicago can be expensive, and traffic congestion is common during peak hours.

Walking:

Chicago is a pedestrian-friendly city with a well-designed street grid. Many of the city's popular attractions, such as Millennium Park, Navy Pier, and the Magnificent Mile, are within walking distance of each other in downtown Chicago. Walking is an excellent way to soak in the city's atmosphere, discover hidden gems, and explore different neighborhoods.

Sightseeing Tours:

Chicago offers various sightseeing tours, including bus tours, boat cruises along the Chicago River, and architectural tours. These guided tours provide informative commentary and allow you to experience the city's landmarks and highlights while enjoying convenient transportation. It's worth noting that Chicago is a large city with heavy traffic at times, particularly during rush hours. Planning your travel routes, and considering factors like distance, time, and congestion, can help you navigate the city more efficiently. Utilizing a combination of transportation options based on your needs and preferences will allow you to explore Chicago conveniently

Unique Transportation Experiences for Both Luxury and Budget Travelers

Chicago offers unique transportation experiences for both luxury and budget travelers. Here are some options tailored to each category:

For Luxury Travelers:

Private Car Services: Luxury travelers can indulge in the comfort and convenience of private car services. Companies like Uber Black and Lyft Lux provide high-end vehicles driven by professional chauffeurs, ensuring a luxurious travel experience throughout the city.

Limousine Services: Renting a limousine allows luxury travelers to explore Chicago in style. Limousine services offer a range of luxurious vehicles equipped with amenities like leather seats, minibars, and entertainment systems. Whether it's a special occasion or simply treating yourself, a limousine ride adds an extra touch of elegance to your transportation.

Helicopter Tours: For a truly unique and breathtaking transportation experience, luxury travelers can opt for helicopter tours. Several companies offer helicopter rides that provide a bird's-eye view of Chicago's iconic skyline and landmarks. It's a luxurious and exhilarating way to see the city from above.

Private Yacht Charters: Chicago's proximity to Lake Michigan makes it possible to enjoy a luxurious private yacht charter. Chartering a yacht allows you to cruise along the lake, taking in stunning views of the cityscape while enjoying premium amenities and personalized service.

Examples are:

The Wendella Boat Tour: This 90-minute tour takes you past some of Chicago's most iconic landmarks, including the Willis Tower, the John Hancock Center, and Millennium Park. You'll also get to see the city from a different perspective, as you cruise along the Chicago River.

The Chicago Architecture Foundation River Cruise: This 90-minute tour takes you past some of Chicago's most famous buildings, including the Tribune Tower, the Wrigley Building, and the Art Institute of Chicago. You'll learn about the history of these buildings and the architects who designed them.

For Budget Travelers:

Chicago Transit Authority (CTA): The CTA offers an affordable way to get around the city. With the use of a reloadable Ventra Card or contactless payment methods, budget travelers can access buses and trains to explore Chicago's neighborhoods, downtown area, and major attractions at a reasonable cost.

Divvy Bikes: Divvy bike-sharing program provides an economical means of transportation for budget-conscious travelers. By purchasing a day pass or single-trip options, you can rent a bike from various stations across the city. It's a fun and environmentally friendly way to navigate Chicago's streets and explore its neighborhoods.

Water Taxis: Chicago's water taxis are a budget-friendly alternative to traditional transportation. These boats operate along the Chicago River and Lake Michigan, offering scenic rides and access to popular destinations like Navy Pier and the Museum Campus at affordable fares. It's a unique way to experience Chicago's waterways while saving money.

Walking Tours: Budget travelers can take advantage of the city's pedestrian-friendly layout by joining walking tours. Many companies offer guided tours that showcase Chicago's history, architecture, and cultural highlights. These tours often operate on a pay-what-you-can or fixed affordable price basis, making them accessible to travelers on a budget.

By considering these unique transportation experiences, both luxury and budget travelers can enjoy their time in Chicago while tailoring their transportation choices to their specific preferences and budgets.

Tips for Getting Around Chicago on a Budget

When navigating Chicago on a budget, consider the following tips to make the most of your money:

Use Public Transportation: The Chicago Transit Authority (CTA) provides a low-cost option for getting about the city. Utilize buses and trains, such as the 'L' train system, to reach various neighborhoods and attractions. Purchase a Ventra Card to take advantage of discounted fares compared to paying cash for each ride. Consider getting a multi-day pass if you plan to use public transportation frequently during your stay.

Walk and Explore on Foot: Chicago is a pedestrian-friendly city with many attractions, parks, and neighborhoods within walking distance of each other, especially in the downtown area. Save money on transportation by exploring the city on foot. You'll also have the opportunity to discover hidden gems and enjoy the city's architecture.

Consider Bike Rentals: Renting a bike through the Divvy bike-sharing program is an affordable and eco-friendly option for navigating Chicago. With numerous bike stations across the city, you can rent a bike for a short period or the entire day. Enjoy biking along the lakefront trails or through the city's neighborhoods while taking in the sights.

Take Advantage of Free Attractions: Chicago offers several free attractions that are worth exploring. Visit Millennium Park to see the iconic Cloud Gate sculpture (also known as "The Bean") or catch a free concert at the Jay Pritzker Pavilion. Lincoln Park Zoo, one of the oldest zoos in the country, is also admission-free. These attractions allow you to enjoy the city's culture and scenery without spending a dime.

Look for Discounted Tickets: Check for discounted tickets or special offers for museums, tours, and other attractions. Many websites, including the official tourism website for Chicago, offer discounted tickets and package deals. Look for coupons or online promotions to save money on entrance fees and activities.

Plan Your Meals Wisely: Dining out can quickly add up, so consider budget-friendly options. Look for local eateries, food trucks, or affordable street food vendors to experience the local cuisine without breaking the bank. Additionally, grocery stores and markets are great for picking up inexpensive snacks or picnic supplies.

Take Advantage of Free Events: Keep an eye out for free events happening in the city during your visit. Chicago hosts various festivals, concerts, and cultural events throughout the year that are often open to the public without an admission fee. Check event calendars and local listings to find free entertainment options.

By following these tips, you can navigate Chicago on a budget while still enjoying its attractions, neighborhoods, and vibrant atmosphere.

Chapter2: Accommodations

Chicago offers a wide range of accommodation options to suit different preferences and budgets. Here are the various types of accommodations available in the city:

Hotels: Chicago boasts a plethora of hotels, ranging from budget-friendly options to luxury establishments. Downtown Chicago is home to many renowned hotels, including those along the Magnificent Mile. These hotels offer amenities such as comfortable rooms, on-site restaurants, and fitness centers, and often provide easy access to popular attractions. The city also has boutique hotels, bed and breakfasts, and extended-stay hotels for those looking for a more unique or long-term stay.

Vacation Rentals: Vacation rentals, such as apartments, condos, and houses, provide a home-away-from-home experience in Chicago. Platforms like Airbnb offer a wide selection of private accommodations throughout the city, allowing visitors to enjoy the comforts of a fully furnished space with amenities like kitchens, living areas, and laundry facilities. Vacation rentals are a popular choice for families, groups, or those seeking a more immersive local experience.

Hostels: For budget-conscious travelers or backpackers, hostels provide affordable accommodation options in Chicago. These shared dormitory-style accommodations offer communal facilities like kitchens, and common areas, and often organize social activities for guests. Hostels are a great way to meet fellow travelers and keep costs low while exploring the city.

Bed and Breakfasts: Chicago has a selection of charming bed and breakfasts, particularly in the city's historic neighborhoods like Lincoln Park and Wicker Park. These smaller accommodations offer a cozy atmosphere and personalized service, often including breakfast as part of the stay. Bed and breakfasts are ideal for those seeking a more intimate and unique lodging experience.

Extended-Stay and Corporate Housing: Visitors planning a longer stay in Chicago can opt for extended-stay accommodations or corporate housing. These furnished apartments or suites are equipped with kitchenettes or full kitchens, allowing guests to enjoy the comforts of home while having the flexibility to cook their meals. Extended-stay options are popular among business travelers, families, and individuals relocating to the city.

Boutique and Design Hotels: Chicago is known for its vibrant art and design scene, and boutique hotels showcase this aesthetic. These smaller, often independently owned hotels offer unique and stylish accommodations, incorporating elements of local culture and design. Boutique hotels provide an intimate and curated experience for travelers looking for something beyond the traditional hotel stay.

Luxury Hotels: Chicago boasts several luxury hotels, offering top-tier amenities, exceptional service, and stunning views of the city. These hotels often feature world-class restaurants, spas, fitness centers, and upscale rooms and suites. Luxury accommodations cater to discerning travelers seeking a lavish and memorable stay.

When choosing accommodation in Chicago, consider factors such as location, budget, amenities, and the type of experience you desire. It's recommended to book in advance, especially during peak travel seasons, to secure the best rates and availability.

Some recommendations for each accommodation option in Chicago:

Hotels:

Budget-Friendly: The Freehand Chicago offers a trendy and affordable stay in a prime downtown location, with shared rooms and private options available.

Mid-Range: The Kinzie Hotel provides a comfortable and modern experience in the heart of River North, with complimentary breakfast and evening receptions.

Luxury: The Peninsula Chicago is a renowned luxury hotel offering exquisite accommodations, exceptional service, and amenities like a rooftop pool and a world-class spa.

Vacation Rentals:

Airbnb: Consider staying in a cozy apartment in the trendy neighborhood of Wicker Park or a stylish condo with a lake view in the vibrant Streeterville area.

Sonder: Sonder offers a selection of professionally managed vacation rentals across Chicago, with options ranging from studios to multi-bedroom apartments in various neighborhoods.

Hostels:

HI, Chicago Hostel is centrally located in the Loop, offering affordable dormitory-style rooms, a complimentary breakfast, and social activities for guests.

Chicago Getaway Hostel in Lincoln Park is a budget-friendly option with clean and comfortable dorms, private rooms, a communal kitchen, and a lively atmosphere.

Bed and Breakfasts:

The Publishing House Bed and Breakfast in West Loop offers elegant rooms, gourmet breakfast, and a welcoming ambiance in a converted historic building.

House of Two Urns Bed and Breakfast in Wicker Park provides charming rooms, a homemade breakfast, and easy access to the neighborhood's trendy shops and restaurants.

Extended-Stay and Corporate Housing:

Oakwood Chicago offers fully furnished apartments in various locations across the city, catering to both short and long-term stays with flexible lease options. Suite Home Chicago provides stylishly furnished apartments in downtown and residential neighborhoods, featuring amenities like full kitchens and on-site fitness centers.

Boutique and Design Hotels:

The Robey in Wicker Park offers a trendy and design-forward experience with stylish rooms, a rooftop lounge, and panoramic views of the city.

The Hoxton Chicago in Fulton Market blends modern design with a vibrant neighborhood atmosphere, featuring comfortable rooms and a lively lobby.

Luxury Hotels:

The Langham, Chicago is a luxurious hotel with lavish accommodations, exceptional service, a spa, and stunning views of the city and the Chicago River.

Waldorf Astoria Chicago provides a luxurious and sophisticated stay in the Gold Coast neighborhood, boasting spacious rooms, a renowned spa, and an upscale restaurant.

These recommendations offer a starting point for exploring the diverse accommodation options available in Chicago, catering to various budgets and preferences. It's always a good idea to research and read reviews to find the best fit for your specific needs and interests.

Tips for Finding the Best Accommodations in Chicago

Finding the top hotels in Chicago may significantly improve your trip experience. Here are some pointers to help you discover the ideal lodging:

Set a Budget: To cut down your possibilities, choose your hotel budget. From budget-friendly hostels to luxury hotels, Chicago has a variety of options to suit all budgets.

Consider Location: Consider the regions you wish to visit as well as the closeness of your lodgings to your sites of interest. While downtown Chicago is a popular option due to its central position and easy access to attractions, other areas such as Lincoln Park and Wicker Park also provide distinct experiences.

Read Reviews: Check out trustworthy travel websites for reviews and ratings to get an idea of the quality and experiences of prior visitors. For the most up-to-date information, pay attention to recent reviews. To make an educated selection, consider both favorable and negative reviews.

Price Comparison: Use online travel agents and hotel booking websites to compare rates and take advantage of any special offers or discounts. Some services even provide price guarantees, assuring that you obtain the best possible pricing.

Examine Amenities: Consider whatever amenities are significant to you. Consider if you need amenities such as a gym, pool, on-site restaurant, or free breakfast. Check that the lodgings have the facilities you need to enjoy your stay.

Look for Package discounts: Some hotels and travel websites offer package discounts that include lodging as well as attractions, excursions, or transportation. These bundles may often provide both savings and convenience.

Consider Other Accommodations: Look into alternatives to standard hotels, such as vacation rentals, bed & breakfasts, and boutique hotels. These solutions may deliver more personalized experiences while also being less expensive.

Book in Advance: It is preferable to book lodgings in advance to ensure the greatest pricing and availability, particularly during high travel seasons or if you have certain dates in mind.

Directly Contact the Accommodation: If you have particular requirements or questions, contact the accommodation directly. They may be able to give further information, special arrangements, or even specific suggestions depending on your need.

Consider Safety and Security: When selecting lodgings, prioritize safety and security. Look for hotels with adequate security measures and take into account guest feedback about safety.

You may get the greatest lodgings in Chicago that meet your budget, interests, and travel requirements by following these guidelines. Take your time researching and comparing choices to ensure a relaxing and pleasurable stay in Chicago.

Unique Accommodations for Both Luxury and Budget Travelers

Chicago offers unique accommodations for both luxury and budget travelers. Here are some options to consider:

Unique Accommodations for Luxury Travelers:

1. The Langham, Chicago: This luxurious hotel occupies a landmark building along the Chicago River. It offers elegant rooms and suites with breathtaking city views, a renowned spa, a rooftop pool, and Michelin-starred dining options.

2. The Peninsula Chicago: Known for its impeccable service, this five-star hotel offers opulent accommodations, a world-class spa, a rooftop terrace with stunning views, and an award-winning restaurant.

3. The Gwen, a Luxury Collection Hotel: Located on the Magnificent Mile, The Gwen showcases a blend of historical and contemporary design. It offers sophisticated rooms, a rooftop terrace, a state-of-the-art fitness center, and a rooftop lounge with panoramic city views.

4. The Robey: Housed in a historic Art Deco building in the trendy Wicker Park

neighborhood, The Robey features stylish rooms, a rooftop lounge with panoramic city views, and a lively atmosphere that captures the spirit of the local community.

Unique Accommodations for Budget Travelers:

1. Urban Holiday Lofts: This budget-friendly hostel in Wicker Park offers shared and private rooms with colorful and eclectic designs. It provides a communal kitchen, a common area with games, and regular social events for guests.

2. HI Chicago Hostel: Situated in the Loop, this centrally located hostel offers affordable dormitory-style rooms, a complimentary breakfast, and organized social activities for guests to mingle and connect.

3. Chicago Getaway Hostel: Located in Lincoln Park, this budget-friendly hostel provides clean and comfortable dorms and private rooms. It offers a communal kitchen, a game

room, and a courtyard where guests can relax and socialize.

4. Freehand Chicago: This trendy and budget-friendly hotel/hostel hybrid in River North offers a variety of room options, including shared and private rooms. It features a communal kitchen, a vibrant bar, and a relaxed atmosphere.

These unique accommodations provide distinct experiences for both luxury and budget travelers. Whether you seek lavish amenities or a more affordable and communal atmosphere, Chicago offers a range of options to cater to your preferences and enhance your stay in the city.

Chapter3: Food and Drinks

Overview of Chicago's Food Scene

Chicago's food and dining scene is renowned for its culinary diversity, innovative chefs, and vibrant restaurant scene. Here's an overview of Chicago's food culture and dining experiences:

Culinary Diversity: Chicago is a melting pot of cultures, and its food scene reflects this diversity. You'll find a wide range of cuisines, from classic American comfort food to ethnic flavors from around the world. The city is particularly known for its deep-dish pizza, Chicago-style hot dogs, Italian beef sandwiches, and diverse culinary neighborhoods like Chinatown, Greektown, and Little Italy.

Michelin-Starred Restaurants: Chicago boasts a remarkable number of Michelin-starred restaurants, recognized for their exceptional quality and creativity. Alinea, Grace, and Acadia are among the esteemed establishments that have earned three Michelin stars. These fine dining experiences showcase cutting-edge techniques and exquisite flavors.

Neighborhood Gems: Beyond the Michelin-starred scene, Chicago is dotted with hidden culinary gems in its various neighborhoods. From family-owned Italian trattorias in Little Italy to hole-in-the-wall taquerias in Pilsen, you can discover a wealth of delicious and authentic dining options off the beaten path.

Food Halls: Chicago's food halls have gained popularity in recent years, offering a wide array of food vendors under one roof. Revival Food Hall, Latinicity, and Time Out Market Chicago are just a few examples. These bustling spaces allow you to sample different cuisines and flavors while enjoying a communal dining atmosphere.

Iconic Eateries: Chicago is home to several iconic eateries that have stood the test of time. Lou Malnati's Pizzeria, Portillo's, and The Billy Goat Tavern are just a few legendary establishments that have become synonymous with the city's culinary identity. Don't miss the chance to savor their classic dishes and experience a taste of Chicago's history.

Craft Breweries and Distilleries: Chicago's craft beer and spirits scene has flourished in recent years. Numerous breweries and distilleries offer tours and tastings, allowing visitors to sample locally brewed beers, spirits, and innovative cocktails. Goose Island Brewery, Revolution Brewing, and KOVAL Distillery are popular choices for beer and spirit enthusiasts.

Farm-to-Table and Sustainable Dining: Chicago embraces the farm-to-table movement, with many restaurants focusing on locally sourced ingredients and sustainable practices. Green City Market, a farmer's market held in Lincoln Park, is an excellent place to explore fresh produce, artisanal products, and sustainable food options.

Food Festivals: Throughout the year, Chicago hosts various food festivals that celebrate the city's culinary offerings. The Taste of Chicago, Chicago Gourmet, and the Chicago Food Truck Festival are just a few examples. These festivals feature an array of food vendors, live entertainment, cooking demonstrations, and a lively atmosphere.

When exploring Chicago's food and dining scene, it's recommended to venture beyond the downtown area and explore different neighborhoods to truly immerse yourself in the city's culinary treasures.

From upscale dining experiences to casual street food, Chicago offers a dynamic and delicious food landscape that is sure to satisfy every palate.

Unique Dining Experiences for Both Luxury and Budget Travelers

Chicago offers unique dining experiences for both luxury and budget travelers. Whether you're looking for an extravagant culinary adventure or seeking affordable yet memorable dining options, the city has something to satisfy every palate. Here are some details on unique dining experiences in Chicago for both luxury and budget travelers:

Luxury Dining Experiences:

1. Alinea: Alinea is a three-Michelin-starred restaurant renowned for its innovative and artistic approach to cuisine. Led by chef Grant Achatz, the restaurant offers a

multi-sensory dining experience with avant-garde dishes and impeccable service.

2. Grace: Grace is another three-Michelin-starred restaurant known for its elegant ambiance and exquisite tasting menus. The restaurant combines bold flavors, unique presentations, and flawless execution to create a memorable fine dining experience.

3. Spiaggia: Spiaggia is a luxurious Italian restaurant located on the Magnificent Mile. Led by award-winning chef Tony Mantuano, it offers a refined dining experience with a focus on authentic Italian flavors and impeccable service.

4. Sixteen: Situated on the 16th floor of the Trump International Hotel, Sixteen offers stunning views of the Chicago skyline along with an exceptional dining experience. The restaurant features a modern American menu

with an emphasis on seasonal ingredients and contemporary culinary techniques.

Budget-Friendly Dining Experiences:

1. Chicago-style Deep-Dish Pizza: For an affordable yet iconic Chicago dining experience, indulge in a slice of deep-dish pizza. Places like Pequod's Pizza, Lou Malnati's, and Giordano's offer delicious deep-dish options that won't break the bank.

2. Maxwell Street Market: Visit Maxwell Street Market, a vibrant street market known for its diverse food stalls offering affordable and authentic street food. From Mexican tacos and Polish sausages to soul food and barbecue, you'll find a variety of flavors to suit your budget.

3. Food Trucks: Chicago's food truck scene has exploded in recent years, offering an array of affordable and delicious eats. Check out popular food truck gatherings like the

Chicago Food Truck Festival or follow individual trucks on social media to track their locations and try their unique offerings.

4. Ethnic Neighborhoods: Chicago's diverse neighborhoods are home to numerous budget-friendly dining options. Explore neighborhoods like Pilsen for delicious Mexican cuisine, Chinatown for affordable dim sum, or Little Italy for traditional Italian dishes at reasonable prices.

5. Diners and Cafés: Chicago has a variety of diners and cafés that offer affordable yet satisfying meals. From classic diners like The Golden Apple to cozy coffee shops like Wormhole Coffee, you can enjoy comfort food, breakfast specialties, and a laid-back atmosphere without breaking the bank.

6. BYOB Restaurants: Look for BYOB (Bring Your Bottle) restaurants in Chicago, where you can bring your alcoholic beverages and

enjoy a meal without the added expense of a high-priced wine or cocktail list. This can be a budget-friendly way to experience the city's dining scene.

Whether you're looking for an extravagant fine dining experience or seeking budget-friendly options, Chicago offers a wide range of unique dining experiences to suit every traveler's taste and budget. From world-class restaurants to street food delights, the city's culinary scene has something to offer everyone.

Best Places to Eat

Chicago is renowned for its diverse culinary scene, offering a wide range of dining options to suit every taste and budget. Here are some of the best places to eat in Chicago, along with their locations and a general idea of their price range:

1. Alinea: Located in Lincoln Park, Alinea is a three-Michelin-starred restaurant known for its avant-garde culinary creations and immersive dining experiences. It offers tasting menus starting at around $300 per person.

2. Girl & the Goat: Situated in the West Loop, Girl & the Goat is a popular restaurant by celebrity chef Stephanie Izard. Known for its creative small plates and bold flavors, it offers a vibrant dining experience with prices ranging from $10 to $30 per dish.

3. The Publican: Found in the Fulton Market District, The Publican is a gastropub specializing in rustic and communal dining. It features a menu inspired by European beer halls, offering a selection of meats, seafood, and seasonal vegetables. Prices range from $15 to $40 per dish.

4. Au Cheval: Located in the West Loop, Au Cheval is famous for its indulgent burgers, along with a variety of comfort food options. Expect to pay around $15 to $20 for a burger or sandwich.

5. Frontera Grill: Situated in River North, Frontera Grill is a highly regarded Mexican restaurant by chef Rick Bayless. It serves authentic and flavorful Mexican dishes, with prices ranging from $15 to $30 per entrée.

6. Lou Malnati's Pizzeria: With multiple locations throughout the city, Lou Malnati's is a beloved institution for deep-dish pizza. Prices for a small deep-dish pizza start around $15.

7. Portillo's: A Chicago classic, Portillo's offers a variety of iconic dishes, including Chicago-style hot dogs and Italian beef sandwiches. Prices are generally affordable,

with hot dogs starting at around $4 and sandwiches around $8 to $10.

8. The Purple Pig: Located in the Magnificent Mile area, The Purple Pig is a Mediterranean-inspired restaurant known for its flavorful small plates and extensive wine list. Prices range from $10 to $25 per dish.

9. Superdawg Drive-In: A Chicago institution since 1948, Superdawg is a classic drive-in serving up delicious hot dogs and other fast food favorites. Prices for a hot dog start at around $5.

Please note that prices are subject to change, and it's advisable to check the restaurant's website or contact them directly for the most accurate and up-to-date information on their menus and prices. Additionally, reservations are recommended for popular establishments, especially those with limited seating capacity.

Nightlife and Entertainment

Chicago's Nightlife, Music and Entertainment Scene

Chicago's nightlife, music, and entertainment scene is vibrant and diverse, offering a wide range of experiences for visitors. From world-class music venues and energetic nightclubs to intimate jazz bars and theatrical performances, the city has something to suit every taste. Here's a glimpse into Chicago's nightlife and entertainment scene, including unique experiences for both luxury and budget travelers:

Nightlife and Music Scene:

Jazz and Blues: Chicago has a rich history in jazz and blues music. Experience the soulful sounds of live jazz at renowned venues like the Green Mill Cocktail Lounge and Andy's Jazz Club. For blues enthusiasts, Kingston Mines and Buddy Guy's

Legends are must-visit destinations to enjoy electrifying live performances.

Music Venues: Chicago boasts iconic music venues that host a wide range of musical genres. The Metro, House of Blues, and The Vic Theatre are popular spots for live concerts featuring both local and international artists. These venues often showcase an eclectic mix of genres, including rock, hip-hop, indie, and electronic music.

Comedy Clubs: Chicago is renowned for its comedy scene, nurturing the talents of famous comedians like Tina Fey and Stephen Colbert. Catch live performances at legendary comedy clubs such as The Second City and Zanies Comedy Club for an evening of laughter and entertainment.

Nightclubs and Dance Halls: For those looking to dance the night away, Chicago offers a vibrant nightclub scene. Clubs like Smart Bar, Sound-Bar, and Studio Paris attract both local and internationally renowned DJs, playing a variety of electronic and dance music genres.

Speakeasies and Craft Cocktails: Chicago is home to numerous speakeasy-style bars that evoke the atmosphere of the Prohibition era. These hidden gems, such as The Violet Hour, The Aviary, and The Berkshire Room, offer meticulously crafted cocktails in stylish and intimate settings.

Unique Experiences for Luxury Travelers:

Chicago Symphony Orchestra: Enjoy a world-class performance by the Grammy Award-winning Chicago Symphony Orchestra at Symphony Center. This renowned ensemble, led by renowned conductors, offers a sophisticated and elegant musical experience.

Broadway in Chicago: Catch a Broadway-quality theater production at one of Chicago's renowned theaters, such as the Cadillac Palace Theatre, Oriental Theatre, or the Chicago Theatre. These venues host a range of hit musicals, plays, and touring productions.

Exclusive Lounge Experiences: Experience Chicago's luxury lounge scene by visiting upscale rooftop bars like the J. Parker or the Cindy's Rooftop. Enjoy panoramic views of the city skyline while sipping on craft cocktails in an elegant and sophisticated setting.

Unique Experiences for Budget Travelers:

Free Outdoor Concerts: During the summer months, Chicago offers numerous free outdoor concerts and music festivals. Millennium Park's Jay Pritzker Pavilion hosts the Grant Park Music Festival, featuring classical and orchestral performances, while the Chicago Blues Festival and the Chicago Jazz Festival showcase talented musicians from around the world.

Improv and Sketch Comedy: Catch affordable improv and sketch comedy shows at theaters like iO Chicago and The Annoyance Theater. These venues offer affordable ticket prices and provide an opportunity to witness emerging comedic talent.

Cultural Events and Festivals: Chicago hosts a variety of cultural events and festivals throughout the year, many of which offer free or low-cost entertainment. From the Chicago Cultural Center's exhibitions and performances to neighborhood festivals celebrating different cultures, you can immerse yourself in the city's vibrant cultural scene without breaking the bank.

These are just a few highlights of Chicago's nightlife, music, and entertainment scene. The city continually offers new and exciting experiences, making it a hub for music lovers, theater enthusiasts, comedy fans, and those seeking a memorable night out on the town.

Tips for Enjoying Nightlife and Entertainment in Chicago on a Budget

If you're looking to enjoy Chicago's nightlife and entertainment scene on a budget, here are some tips to make the most of your experience:

1. Explore Free Events: Keep an eye out for free events happening in the city, especially during the summer months. From outdoor concerts and festivals to art exhibitions and cultural performances, Chicago offers a wide

range of free entertainment options. Check out Millennium Park's event calendar, neighborhood festivals, and community events for budget-friendly entertainment.

2. Happy Hour Specials: Take advantage of happy hour specials offered by bars and restaurants throughout the city. Many establishments offer discounted drinks and food during specific hours, allowing you to enjoy a night out without breaking the bank. Research local bars and their happy hour timings to find the best deals.

3. Comedy Clubs: Chicago is known for its thriving comedy scene, and many comedy clubs offer affordable ticket prices, especially on weeknights or for early shows. Look for discounted tickets, group rates, or special promotions to catch a hilarious performance at a lower cost.

4. Neighborhood Bars and Pubs: Explore local neighborhood bars and pubs, which often offer a more relaxed and affordable atmosphere compared to trendy nightclubs. These establishments frequently have drink specials, trivia nights, or live music performances, providing an enjoyable evening without spending a fortune.

5. BYOB Restaurants: Save on pricey drinks by opting for BYOB (Bring Your Bottle) restaurants. These establishments allow you to bring your alcoholic beverages, which can significantly reduce your dining expenses while still enjoying a delicious meal.

6. Off-Peak Hours: Consider visiting popular attractions and entertainment venues during off-peak hours. Some venues may offer discounted admission or ticket prices during quieter times, allowing you to enjoy the experience while saving money.

7. Explore Street Performances: Chicago's streets often come alive with talented street performers showcasing their skills in music, dance, and other artistic performances. Take a stroll along Michigan Avenue, Navy Pier, or the Magnificent Mile, and enjoy the vibrant street entertainment without spending a dime.

8. Check Online Deals: Look for online deals, discounts, and promotional offers for entertainment and nightlife experiences in Chicago. Websites like Groupon and LivingSocial often feature discounted tickets or packages for various shows, performances, and attractions.

9. Public Events and Gatherings: Keep an eye out for public events and gatherings that offer free or low-cost entertainment. From outdoor movie screenings in parks to cultural parades and street festivals, these events provide a lively and budget-friendly experience.

10. Plan Ahead: Research and plan your outings to make the most of your budget. Look for affordable options, plan your itinerary around happy hours and free events, and consider purchasing any necessary tickets or passes online in advance to potentially secure better deals.

By following these tips, you can enjoy Chicago's nightlife and entertainment scene on a budget without compromising on the fun and excitement the city has to offer.

Chapter4: Attractions and Activities

Chicago's Top Attractions

Chicago, the vibrant and culturally rich city in the heart of the United States, is brimming with iconic attractions that captivate visitors from around the world. From stunning architecture and world-class museums to beautiful parks and vibrant neighborhoods, here are some of the major highlights of Chicago's top attractions:

Willis Tower Skydeck: Formerly known as the Sears Tower, the Willis Tower stands tall as an architectural masterpiece and an emblem of Chicago's skyline. The Skydeck, located on the 103rd floor, offers panoramic views of the city and beyond. Step onto the glass ledge, known as "The Ledge," for a thrilling experience high above the bustling streets.

Navy Pier: Situated along Lake Michigan, Navy Pier is a bustling entertainment destination that offers something for everyone. Take a ride on the iconic Ferris wheel and enjoy breathtaking views of the city and the lake. Explore the diverse array of attractions, including the Chicago Children's Museum, IMAX Theater, boat tours, restaurants, shops, and live entertainment. Navy Pier also hosts spectacular fireworks displays during the summer months.

Millennium Park: This urban oasis in downtown Chicago has become an iconic gathering place. Admire the mesmerizing Cloud Gate sculpture, lovingly referred to as "The Bean," which reflects the city's skyline and offers unique photo opportunities. The Jay Pritzker Pavilion, an outdoor concert venue, hosts free summer concerts and performances. Visit the Crown Fountain, where you can cool off in the interactive reflecting pool and witness the playful digital faces projected onto the tower's LED screens.

Art Institute of Chicago: As one of the oldest and largest art museums in the United States, the Art Institute of Chicago is a treasure trove of artistic masterpieces. Wander through its vast halls and discover renowned works of art from around the world. Marvel at iconic pieces such as Grant Wood's "American Gothic," Vincent van Gogh's "The Bedroom," and Georges Seurat's "A Sunday on La Grande Jatte." The museum also features ancient Egyptian and Greek artifacts, contemporary art, and rotating exhibitions.

Museum Campus: Located along Lake Michigan, the Museum Campus is a picturesque park that houses three world-class museums. Explore the Field Museum, home to Sue, the largest and most complete Tyrannosaurus rex fossil ever discovered.

Visit the Shedd Aquarium to admire a diverse array of marine life, including beluga whales, dolphins, and penguins. Delve into the wonders of the universe at the Adler Planetarium, where interactive exhibits and immersive shows take you on a journey through space.

Magnificent Mile: A shopper's paradise, the Magnificent Mile stretches along Michigan Avenue and is lined with luxury boutiques, department stores, and renowned designer brands. Indulge in retail therapy, dine at world-class restaurants, and admire the architectural gems that dot the avenue. Don't miss the historic Water Tower, one of the few buildings to survive the Great Chicago Fire of 1871.

Lincoln Park Zoo: Nestled within the expansive Lincoln Park, this free-admission zoo offers an enchanting escape from the urban hustle. Explore a diverse range of animals, including lions, giraffes, monkeys, and polar bears. The zoo also features a nature boardwalk and a farm-in-the-zoo where children can interact with domestic animals.

Garfield Park Conservatory: Located on the city's West Side, the Garfield Park Conservatory is a haven of natural beauty. Explore its vast collection of rare and exotic plants showcased within stunning indoor gardens. Marvel at the Palm House, Fern Room, and Desert House, each with its own unique atmosphere and plant species.

Chicago Riverwalk: Take a stroll along the Chicago Riverwalk and soak in the scenic views of the city skyline and the river's gentle flow. The Riverwalk offers a vibrant mix of restaurants, cafes, and outdoor seating, making it the perfect spot to relax, enjoy a meal, or embark on a scenic boat tour along the Chicago River.

Wrigley Field: Baseball fans shouldn't miss the opportunity to visit Wrigley Field, the historic home of the Chicago Cubs. Immerse yourself in the rich history of America's favorite pastime as you cheer on the Cubs during a game or take a guided tour of the stadium to learn about its storied past.

Chicago Cultural Center: The Chicago Cultural Center is an art and cultural center housed in a gorgeous historic edifice. Explore the amazing architecture, including the Tiffany glass dome, and take in a range of exhibits, concerts, film screenings, and talks. The facility also has the biggest Tiffany stained-glass dome in the world, a real creative masterpiece.

360 Chicago Observation Deck: Located in the iconic John Hancock Center, the 360 Chicago Observation Deck offers stunning 360-degree views of the city skyline and Lake Michigan. Take a ride

on the thrilling TILT, a glass-enclosed platform that tilts outward from the building, providing a unique perspective on the city below.

Museum of Science and Industry: Situated in the historic Hyde Park neighborhood, the Museum of Science and Industry offers interactive exhibits that educate and entertain visitors of all ages. Explore hands-on displays on technology, engineering, space exploration, and more. Don't miss the chance to step inside a U-505 submarine or witness a simulated tornado in the Science Storms exhibit.

Chicago Architecture River Cruise: Embark on a river cruise to discover Chicago's stunning architecture from a unique perspective. Knowledgeable guides narrate the history and significance of the city's renowned buildings as you sail along the Chicago River. It's a fantastic way to admire the skyline and learn about Chicago's architectural heritage.

Hyde Park: Located on the city's South Side, Hyde Park is a vibrant neighborhood that boasts cultural landmarks such as the University of Chicago and the Museum of Science and Industry. Stroll through beautiful parks, explore independent bookstores and cafes, and immerse yourself in the intellectual atmosphere of this historic neighborhood.

From towering skyscrapers and world-class museums to picturesque parks and vibrant neighborhoods, Chicago's top attractions offer a diverse range of experiences for visitors to enjoy. Whether you're drawn to the city's architectural marvels, its rich cultural heritage, or its natural beauty, there's something for everyone to discover in the Windy City.

Exciting Activities

Chicago offers a multitude of exciting activities for outdoor enthusiasts, sports lovers, and those seeking recreational adventures. Here are some of the best activities to do in Chicago in terms of outdoor activities, sports, and recreation:

Bike along Lakefront Trail: Explore the scenic beauty of Lake Michigan by biking along the Lakefront Trail. This 18-mile path stretches along the lake, offering stunning views of the water, beaches, and Chicago's skyline. Rent a bike and enjoy a leisurely ride or join a guided bike tour to discover the city's highlights.

Visit Millennium Park: Enjoy the outdoors at Millennium Park, where you can take a stroll, have a picnic, or simply relax in the beautiful surroundings. Don't miss the Crown Fountain, where interactive water displays and digital art create a unique experience.

Kayak on the Chicago River: Experience Chicago from a different perspective by kayaking on the Chicago River. Join a guided kayak tour or rent a kayak and paddle through the city's waterways, marveling at the architectural gems that line the riverbanks.

Explore the 606 Trail: Formerly an elevated railway line, the 606 Trail has been transformed into an elevated park and recreational trail. Walk, jog, or bike along this urban oasis, enjoying the green spaces, art installations, and vibrant neighborhoods it connects.

Attend a Chicago Cubs or Chicago White Sox Game: Chicago is a sports-crazed city, and baseball fans can catch a game at either Wrigley Field, home of the Chicago Cubs, or Guaranteed Rate Field, home of the Chicago White Sox. Immerse yourself in the lively atmosphere and cheer on the home team.

Play Beach Volleyball at North Avenue Beach: Join a game of beach volleyball or simply soak up the sun at North Avenue Beach. Located on the shores of Lake Michigan, this popular beach offers stunning views of the city skyline and is a hub of activity during the summer months.

Picnic at Grant Park: Head to Grant Park, also known as "Chicago's Front Yard," for a relaxing picnic. Spread out a blanket on the lush green lawns and enjoy the picturesque surroundings, with landmarks such as Buckingham Fountain and the Art Institute of Chicago within sight.

Take a Boat Tour on Lake Michigan: Explore the vastness of Lake Michigan on a boat tour. Choose from architectural cruises, sunset cruises, or even fireworks cruises, and marvel at the stunning skyline while learning about the city's history and architecture.

Golf at Jackson Park Golf Course: Golf enthusiasts can tee off at the scenic Jackson Park Golf Course, which offers 18 holes surrounded by lush greenery and panoramic views of Lake Michigan. Enjoy a challenging round of golf in a serene setting.

Visit Lincoln Park Zoo: Take a break from the city's hustle and bustle and immerse yourself in nature at Lincoln Park Zoo. This free-admission zoo is home to a variety of animals and offers a peaceful escape with beautifully landscaped gardens and walking paths.

Engage in WaterSports at Montrose Beach: Montrose Beach is a popular spot for water sports enthusiasts. Rent a kayak, paddleboard, or jet ski and enjoy the thrill of gliding across the water. You can also join a beach yoga class or simply relax on the sandy shores.

Attend an Outdoor Concert or Festival: Chicago hosts numerous outdoor concerts and festivals throughout the year. From the Taste of Chicago food festival to the Chicago Blues Festival, there's always something happening that celebrates music, art, food, and culture.

These activities showcase the diverse range of outdoor adventures, sports, and recreational opportunities available in Chicago.

Unique Attractions and Activities for Both Luxury and Budget Travelers

Chicago offers a wide range of unique attractions and activities that cater to both luxury and budget travelers. Here are some suggestions for unique experiences that can be enjoyed regardless of your travel budget:

Luxury:

- Take a Helicopter Tour: Treat yourself to a thrilling helicopter tour over Chicago's skyline. Admire the city's iconic landmarks, such as Willis Tower, Navy Pier, and Millennium Park, from a bird's-eye perspective.
- Indulge in Fine Dining: Chicago is renowned for its culinary scene. Experience luxury dining at Michelin-starred restaurants such as Alinea, Spiaggia, or Acadia, where

world-class chefs create unforgettable gastronomic experiences.

- Enjoy a Spa Day: Pamper yourself with a luxurious spa day at one of Chicago's upscale wellness retreats. From rejuvenating massages to soothing facials, indulge in relaxation and self-care at renowned spas like The Peninsula Chicago or The Langham Chicago.

- Attend a Broadway Show: Catch a world-class Broadway production at one of Chicago's renowned theaters, such as the Oriental Theatre or the Cadillac Palace Theatre. Immerse yourself in the magic of live performances and witness top-notch talent on stage.

Budget:

- Explore Street Art in Wicker Park: Wander through the vibrant neighborhood of Wicker

Park and admire its street art scene. Murals and graffiti art adorn the walls, providing a colorful and dynamic backdrop for your explorations.

- Attend Free Cultural Events: Chicago hosts a variety of free cultural events throughout the year. From summer music festivals like the Chicago Blues Festival to the Taste of Chicago food festival, you can immerse yourself in the city's cultural offerings without breaking the bank.

- Visit Free Museums: Take advantage of the city's many free museum days. The Art Institute of Chicago offers free admission to Illinois residents on certain weekdays, and the Museum of Contemporary Art offers free admission on Tuesdays for all visitors.

- Enjoy Lakefront Activities: Chicago's lakefront is a playground for outdoor enthusiasts. Take a stroll along the Lakefront

Trail, have a picnic in one of the lakeside parks, or relax on the beaches. These activities offer stunning views and are completely free of charge.

- Attend Neighborhood Festivals: Explore Chicago's diverse neighborhoods and attend their lively street festivals. From the Mexican Independence Day Parade in Pilsen to the Andersonville Arts Fest, these events showcase the unique culture and traditions of each neighborhood and often feature local artists, musicians, and food vendors.

Both luxury and budget travelers can find unique attractions and activities in Chicago that cater to their preferences. Whether you're seeking upscale experiences or looking to explore the city on a budget, Chicago has something for everyone to enjoy.

Day Trips and Excursions

Chicago's central location and excellent transportation links make it an ideal base for day trips and excursions to nearby attractions. Here is an overview of some popular day trips and excursions that you can take from Chicago:

Milwaukee, Wisconsin: Located just 90 miles north of Chicago, Milwaukee offers a vibrant cultural scene, historic architecture, and renowned breweries. Explore the Milwaukee Art Museum, visit the Harley-Davidson Museum, or take a brewery tour to sample local craft beers.

Starved Rock State Park: Located about 100 miles southwest of Chicago, Starved Rock State Park is a natural oasis of stunning canyons, waterfalls, and hiking trails. Spend the day exploring the park, taking in breathtaking views, and enjoying outdoor activities like hiking, fishing, and picnicking.

Lake Geneva, Wisconsin: Approximately 80 miles northwest of Chicago, Lake Geneva is a charming resort town known for its beautiful lake, historic mansions, and outdoor recreational opportunities. Take a boat tour on the lake, visit the Black Point Estate, or indulge in water sports like kayaking and paddleboarding.

Indiana Dunes National Park: Situated along the southern shore of Lake Michigan, Indiana Dunes National Park is just a short drive from Chicago. Explore its scenic beaches, dunes, and hiking trails. Enjoy swimming, bird-watching, or simply relaxing in the picturesque surroundings.

Galena, Illinois: Located about 165 miles northwest of Chicago, Galena is a historic town renowned for its well-preserved 19th-century buildings and charming Main Street. Stroll through the town's shops, visit historic sites like the Ulysses S. Grant Home, or take a scenic drive along the Great River Road.

Frank Lloyd Wright's Home and Studio: Located in Oak Park, just outside of Chicago, Frank Lloyd Wright's Home and Studio is a must-visit for architecture enthusiasts. Take a guided tour to explore the iconic architect's former residence and see where he developed his revolutionary design concepts.

Illinois Beach State Park: Situated along Lake Michigan, Illinois Beach State Park offers sandy beaches, hiking trails, and camping facilities. Enjoy swimming, sunbathing, or hiking through the park's diverse ecosystems.

Chicago Botanic Garden: Located in Glencoe, a northern suburb of Chicago, the Chicago Botanic

Garden is a peaceful retreat with stunning gardens, walking paths, and seasonal flower displays. Explore the 385-acre garden, attend a workshop or lecture, and enjoy the tranquility of nature.

The Morton Arboretum: Situated in Lisle, just west of Chicago, The Morton Arboretum is a beautiful outdoor space featuring a vast collection of trees, gardens, and nature trails. Walk or bike through the arboretum, participate in educational programs, or enjoy seasonal events such as the Illumination light display.

Route 66 Road Trip: Embark on a nostalgic road trip along the historic Route 66, which starts in Chicago. Drive through charming towns, visit roadside attractions, and soak in the Americana atmosphere of this iconic highway.

These day trips and excursions from Chicago offer a range of experiences, from exploring nature to immersing yourself in history and culture. Whether you're seeking outdoor adventures, architectural wonders, or a change of scenery, these destinations provide enjoyable options just a short distance from the bustling city of Chicago.

Shopping

Chicago's Shopping Scene

Chicago boasts a vibrant shopping scene with a variety of options for both souvenirs and market experiences. Here's an overview of Chicago's shopping scene:

Magnificent Mile: Located on Michigan Avenue, the Magnificent Mile is Chicago's premier shopping destination. This iconic stretch is lined with luxury boutiques, flagship stores, and high-end designer brands. Here, you'll find renowned department stores like Nordstrom, Bloomingdale's, and Saks Fifth Avenue, as well as upscale retailers like Gucci, Tiffany & Co., and Louis Vuitton.

State Street: State Street is another popular shopping district in downtown Chicago. It offers a mix of department stores, trendy retailers, and affordable fashion options. Check out Macy's on State Street, which occupies an entire city block and is famous for its stunning architecture and extensive product selection.

Chicago's Neighborhoods: Explore Chicago's diverse neighborhoods for a unique shopping experience. In Wicker Park and Bucktown, you'll find independent boutiques, vintage shops, and local designers. Andersonville is known for its specialty stores and eclectic shops, while Lincoln Park's

Armitage Avenue features upscale fashion and home decor stores.

Oak Street: For luxury shopping, head to Oak Street in the Gold Coast neighborhood. This charming street is lined with high-end designer boutiques, including Prada, Hermès, and Jimmy Choo. You'll also find luxury department stores like Barney's New York and boutique jewelry stores.

Chicago's Markets:

The Chicago French Market: Located in the West Loop, this bustling indoor market offers a wide range of gourmet food vendors, artisanal products, and specialty items. Explore the diverse culinary offerings, sample international cuisines, and pick up unique gifts and souvenirs.

Randolph Street Market: Held monthly, the Randolph Street Market is a must-visit for vintage enthusiasts. Browse through an array of antique treasures, vintage clothing, furniture, and collectibles. The market also features live music, food vendors, and a festive atmosphere.

Maxwell Street Market: This historic open-air market is a Chicago institution. Located on the Near West Side, the market offers a mix of new and used goods, including clothing, electronics, household items, and street food. It's a vibrant and culturally diverse market experience.

Souvenirs:
Chicago-themed Apparel: Look for T-shirts, hoodies, and accessories adorned with the iconic Chicago skyline, sports team logos, or famous landmarks like the Bean (Cloud Gate) in Millennium

Park. You can find them at souvenir shops throughout the city.

Chicago Food Specialties: Bring home a taste of Chicago with deep-dish pizza kits, gourmet popcorn, Chicago-style hot dogs, or locally-made chocolates. Visit specialty food shops like Garrett Popcorn Shops, Lou Malnati's, or the Fannie May chocolate stores.

Art and Crafts: Support local artists and artisans by purchasing unique artwork, pottery, jewelry, or handmade crafts. Check out art galleries and boutiques in neighborhoods like Pilsen, West Loop, and Andersonville.

Chicago's shopping scene offers something for everyone, from luxury brands and high-end retailers to unique markets and locally crafted souvenirs.

Unique Shopping Experiences for Both Luxury and Budget Travelers

Chicago offers unique shopping experiences for both luxury and budget travelers. Here are some suggestions to cater to different preferences and budgets:

Luxury Shopping Experiences:

The Shops at North Bridge: Located on Michigan Avenue, The Shops at North Bridge is an upscale shopping destination that features luxury brands such as Gucci, Burberry, and Louis Vuitton. Enjoy a luxurious shopping experience in a sophisticated atmosphere.

Oak Street: Head to Oak Street in the Gold Coast neighborhood for a luxury shopping spree. This prestigious street is home to high-end designer boutiques, including Prada, Hermès, and Jimmy

Choo. Indulge in luxury fashion, accessories, and jewelry in a refined setting.

The 900 North Michigan Shops: Situated on the Magnificent Mile, the 900 North Michigan Shops offer a collection of luxury retailers, including Bloomingdale's, Max Mara, and J.Crew. Explore the upscale shops, indulge in designer fashion, and enjoy the elevated shopping ambiance.

Budget-Friendly Shopping Experiences:
Andersonville: Explore the Andersonville neighborhood, known for its unique shops and independent boutiques. Discover vintage clothing stores, locally made crafts, and specialty shops offering affordable yet distinctive items.

Fashion Outlets of Chicago: Located near O'Hare International Airport, the Fashion Outlets of Chicago is a haven for budget-conscious shoppers.

Browse through a wide range of designer and brand-name stores, including Nike, Gap, and Coach, where you can find discounted prices and great deals.

Chicago's Neighborhood Thrift Stores: Embark on a thrift store adventure in neighborhoods like Wicker Park, Logan Square, and Lakeview. These areas are known for their thrift and vintage shops, where you can score unique clothing pieces, accessories, and home decor items at budget-friendly prices.

Unique Shopping Experiences for All:
The Chicago Pedway: Explore the underground Pedway system, which connects various buildings and shopping centers in downtown Chicago. Discover a mix of shops, boutiques, and eateries while navigating through the underground tunnels, providing a unique shopping experience away from the bustling streets.

Local Art Markets and Pop-up Shops: Keep an eye out for local art markets and pop-up shops that showcase the work of independent artists and artisans. These temporary markets often feature handmade crafts, artwork, and unique products, allowing you to support local talent and find one-of-a-kind treasures.

Chicago Antique Markets: Visit antique markets like the Randolph Street Market or the Vintage Garage Chicago. These markets offer a wide array of vintage and antique items, including furniture, clothing, accessories, and collectibles. You can find unique pieces with historical charm at affordable prices.

Chicago's shopping scene caters to all budgets and preferences, ensuring that both luxury and budget travelers can find unique and enjoyable shopping experiences. Whether you're looking for high-end luxury brands, budget-friendly finds, or one-of-a-kind treasures, Chicago has it all. Take advantage of the city's diverse neighborhoods, markets, and shopping districts to discover the perfect shopping experience for you.

Chapter 5: Major Tips and Itinerary

Health and Safety Tips

It is critical to prioritize your health and safety while traveling to any place, especially Chicago. Here are some important health and safety considerations to remember throughout your visit:

Keep Up to Date: Keep up to speed with the most recent travel warnings and guidance issued by health authorities and local government bodies. Keep up to date on any special safety precautions or restrictions that may be in effect during your stay in Chicago.

Personal Safety: Although Chicago is typically a safe city, conventional measures should be taken. Be cautious of your surroundings, particularly if you're in a busy place or at night. Keep your stuff safe and avoid exhibiting precious goods or huge quantities of cash. When wandering or touring the city, stick to well-lit and crowded areas.

transit Safety: Keep an eye on your stuff and be wary of pickpockets while utilizing public transit. Use trustworthy transportation companies and authorized taxi services. Before entering a ride-sharing car, confirm the driver and vehicle details. When walking, obey traffic laws and utilize crosswalks.

remain Hydrated: Because Chicago has hot and humid summers, it's critical to remain hydrated, particularly while spending time outside. Carry a water bottle with you at all times and drink lots of fluids, even if you don't feel thirsty. This is particularly vital while participating in outdoor activities or touring.

Sun Protection: Wear sunscreen with a high SPF, a hat, sunglasses, and lightweight, breathable clothes to protect yourself from the sun's damaging rays. Seek shade during the warmest parts of the day (often between 10 a.m. and 4 p.m.).

Culinary and Water Safety: Chicago boasts a bustling culinary scene, but when it comes to food and water safety, it's crucial to be cautious. Ensure that the meal is properly prepared and cooked. If you are concerned, drink bottled water or use a dependable water filtration system to avoid drinking tap water.

Emergency Services: Learn how to call the local police, fire department, and medical services in case of an emergency. Don't be afraid to seek medical treatment if you have any health problems.

Consider getting travel insurance that includes coverage for medical bills, trip cancellation or interruption, and personal possessions. This may give peace of mind as well as financial security in the event of unanticipated situations.

Stay in the Following Areas: While there are numerous safe neighborhoods in Chicago, it's best to stick to well-known and suggested locations, particularly if you're new to the city. Investigate your lodging options and choose reputed facilities in secure areas.

Remember that your health and safety are of the utmost importance throughout your stay in Chicago. You can assure a seamless and pleasurable trip while seeing the city's attractions and immersing yourself in its lively culture by following these important health and safety precautions.

Tips for Planning Day Trips and Excursions on a Budget

Planning day trips and excursions on a budget can be a great way to explore the surroundings of Chicago without breaking the bank. Here are some tips to help you plan affordable day trips and excursions:

1. Research and Plan Ahead: Before embarking on any day trip or excursion, do thorough

research to find affordable options. Look for attractions or destinations that offer free or low-cost admission, discounts, or special offers. Check websites, travel forums, and local tourism resources for budget-friendly recommendations.

2. Public Transportation: Utilize public transportation options like buses or trains to reach your day trip destinations. Public transportation is often more cost-effective compared to renting a car or booking private transportation. Check the schedules, routes, and fares in advance to ensure a smooth journey.

3. Pack Your Meals: Bringing your meals and snacks can significantly cut down on expenses during day trips. Pack a picnic lunch or opt for a grocery store stop to pick up affordable food items. This way, you can

enjoy a meal without relying on expensive restaurants or eateries.

4. Group Discounts and Coupons: If you're traveling with a group, look for group discounts or discounted packages available for attractions or activities. Additionally, search for coupons or promo codes that offer savings on entrance fees or services. These discounts can help reduce overall expenses.

5. Take Advantage of Free Attractions: Many destinations have free attractions or points of interest that you can explore without spending any money. Research free parks, gardens, viewpoints, or historical sites in the area and include them in your itinerary. These can provide memorable experiences at no cost.

6. Opt for Nature and Outdoor Activities: Explore the natural beauty and outdoor spaces surrounding Chicago. Visit local

parks, hiking trails, or beaches that offer free or low-cost access. Enjoy activities like picnicking, hiking, swimming, or biking, which are often budget-friendly and provide a chance to connect with nature.

7. Seek Local Recommendations: Talk to locals or seek advice from online forums or travel communities for budget-friendly day trip ideas. Locals often have insider knowledge of lesser-known attractions or hidden gems that are affordable and offer a unique experience.

8. Consider Self-Guided Tours: Instead of booking expensive guided tours, opt for self-guided tours using travel apps, online resources, or guidebooks. These resources provide information and maps, allowing you to explore at your own pace and save money on guided tour fees.

9. Look for Package Deals: Some attractions or tour operators offer package deals that

include multiple activities or attractions at a discounted price. Look for bundled offers that can save you money compared to booking individual experiences.

10. Plan for Additional Expenses: While planning your day trips, consider any additional expenses such as parking fees, equipment rentals, or souvenirs. Allocate a budget for these expenses to avoid any surprises and ensure you stay within your planned budget.

By following these tips, you can plan enjoyable and budget-friendly day trips and excursions from Chicago. With careful research, smart choices, and a little creativity, you can make the most of your budget while exploring the surrounding areas and creating memorable experiences.

Tips for Saving Money on Attractions and Activities

When visiting Chicago, saving money on attractions and activities can help stretch your budget and allow you to experience more during your trip. Here are some tips for saving money on attractions and activities:

1. Research Free or Discounted Days: Many attractions in Chicago offer free or discounted admission on specific days or times. Research the attractions you want to visit and check if they have any promotional offers or discounted entries on certain days.

2. City Passes and Discount Cards: Consider purchasing city passes or discount cards that offer bundled access to multiple attractions at a discounted price. Examples include the Chicago CityPASS or the Go Chicago Card. These passes often provide significant

savings and can be a cost-effective way to visit popular attractions.

3. Look for Online Deals and Coupons: Before purchasing tickets, search for online deals, promotions, and coupons. Check the official websites of attractions, as well as deal websites and travel platforms for any ongoing discounts or special offers. You might find discounted prices, buy-one-get-one-free deals, or package deals that save you money.

4. Take Advantage of Free Attractions: Chicago has a variety of free attractions and points of interest that you can explore without spending a dime. Visit Millennium Park, where you can see the iconic Cloud Gate sculpture (also known as "The Bean") and enjoy free concerts and events. Explore the Navy Pier, Lincoln Park Zoo, or the Art Institute of Chicago on their free admission days.

5. Consider Alternative Attractions: Chicago offers a range of attractions beyond the well-known tourist spots. Explore lesser-known museums, galleries, or cultural centers that offer affordable or donation-based entry fees. These off-the-beaten-path attractions can provide unique experiences without the high costs.

6. Check for Student or Senior Discounts: If you're a student or a senior, inquire about any discounted rates available at attractions. Many museums and attractions offer reduced prices for students or senior citizens, so don't forget to bring your valid ID or membership card.

7. Take Advantage of Free Guided Tours: Some attractions offer free guided tours as part of the admission fee. Make use of these guided tours to enhance your experience and gain

insights from knowledgeable guides without paying extra for a separate tour.

8. Explore Free Cultural Events: Keep an eye out for free cultural events happening in Chicago during your visit. Check event calendars for concerts, festivals, art exhibits, or outdoor performances that offer free entry. These events not only provide entertainment but also give you a chance to immerse yourself in the local culture.

9. Consider DIY Sightseeing: Instead of booking expensive guided tours, consider exploring the city on your own. Use public transportation or walk to popular landmarks and neighborhoods. Research self-guided tours or download travel apps that offer audio guides or suggested itineraries for self-exploration.

10. Follow Social Media and Newsletters: Stay connected with attractions by following them

on social media platforms or subscribing to their newsletters. They often share exclusive discounts, promotions, or last-minute deals that can help you save money on admission fees or activities.

By implementing these tips, you can save money on attractions and activities in Chicago, allowing you to make the most of your visit without exceeding your budget.

Tips for Finding the Best Deals on Shopping

When it comes to finding the best deals on shopping in Chicago, consider the following tips to help you save money:

1. Research and Compare Prices: Before making any purchase, research prices online and compare them across different retailers. Use price comparison websites or apps to

find the best deals on specific products. This will give you a better understanding of the average price range and help you identify the most affordable options.

2. Shop During Sale Seasons: Keep an eye on seasonal sales, such as Black Friday, Cyber Monday, or end-of-season clearance sales. These periods offer significant discounts and promotions across a wide range of products. Plan your shopping accordingly to take advantage of these sales and maximize your savings.

3. Visit Outlet Malls and Discount Stores: Explore outlet malls or discount stores in and around Chicago. These establishments offer brand-name products at discounted prices. You can find clothing, accessories, electronics, and more at reduced rates compared to regular retail stores.

4. Utilize Coupons and Promo Codes: Look for coupons and promo codes that can be used both online and in-store. Retailers often provide discounts or special offers through these codes. Websites, apps, or even newspapers can be sources for finding these money-saving coupons.

5. Follow Social Media and Apps: Follow your favorite retailers and brands on social media platforms. Many companies announce flash sales, limited-time discounts, or exclusive offers through their social media channels. Additionally, consider using shopping apps that provide cashback or rewards for your purchases.

6. Consider Secondhand or Thrift Shopping: Explore thrift stores, consignment shops, or online platforms for secondhand shopping. You can find unique and affordable items at significantly lower prices than buying them

new. It's a sustainable and budget-friendly way to shop.

7. Timing Matters: Timing your shopping can lead to better deals. For example, shop for winter clothing at the end of the winter season when stores are clearing out inventory for spring items. Similarly, shop for swimwear at the end of summer when prices are reduced for next year's stock.

8. Negotiate and Bargain: In certain markets or independent stores, bargaining or negotiating prices is accepted. Don't hesitate to ask for a better price, especially if you're purchasing multiple items or if the product has slight imperfections. Polite and friendly negotiation can sometimes lead to discounts.

9. Consider Tax-Free Shopping: If you're an international traveler, be aware of the tax refund schemes available in Chicago. Some stores offer tax-free shopping for tourists,

allowing you to get a refund on the sales tax paid on eligible purchases. Familiarize yourself with the process and requirements to take advantage of this opportunity.

By applying these tips, you can find the best deals on shopping in Chicago.

Suggested itinerary

Here are three suggested itineraries for exploring Chicago based on different interests and durations of stay:

1. Classic Chicago Experience (3 Days):

Day 1:

- Morning: Start your day by visiting Millennium Park and taking a selfie at the iconic Cloud Gate sculpture ("The Bean"). Explore the park and enjoy the beautiful landscape.

- Afternoon: Head to the Art Institute of Chicago, one of the world's premier art museums. Spend the afternoon admiring the vast collection of artworks from various periods and cultures.
- Evening: Take a stroll along the Magnificent Mile, Chicago's famous shopping district. Enjoy the vibrant atmosphere, browse through upscale stores, and dine at one of the many restaurants in the area.

Day 2:

- Morning: Visit the Willis Tower Skydeck for breathtaking views of the city from the observation deck. "The Ledge," a glass balcony that stretches out from the structure, is a must-see..
- Afternoon: Explore Navy Pier, a popular entertainment destination. Enjoy rides at the amusement park, take a boat tour on Lake

Michigan, and indulge in local snacks like popcorn or Chicago-style hot dogs.

- Evening: Immerse yourself in the vibrant nightlife of Chicago by visiting one of the city's renowned jazz clubs or comedy venues. Enjoy live performances and experience the city's cultural scene.

Day 3:

- Morning: Discover the history and architecture of Chicago with an architecture boat tour along the Chicago River. Learn about the city's iconic buildings and their architectural significance.
- Afternoon: Explore the Museum Campus, home to three world-class museums: the Field Museum, Shedd Aquarium, and Adler Planetarium. Choose one or visit all three to delve into natural history, marine life, and astronomy.

- Evening: Wrap up your Chicago experience by enjoying a delicious deep-dish pizza, a local specialty. Choose from various renowned pizzerias in the city and savor this classic Chicago dish.

Family-Friendly Adventure (5 Days):

Day 1:

- Morning: Start your day at Lincoln Park Zoo, a free zoo with a wide variety of animals. Enjoy family-friendly exhibits and educational programs.
- Afternoon: Visit the Chicago Children's Museum at Navy Pier, offering interactive exhibits and play areas for kids of all ages.
- Evening: Enjoy a family dinner at one of the family-friendly restaurants in the city, such as the Rainforest Cafe or the Chicago Diner.

Day 2:

- Morning: Spend the day at the Museum of Science and Industry, where kids can engage in interactive exhibits, and hands-on experiments, and learn about various scientific disciplines.

- Afternoon: Explore Maggie Daley Park, a sprawling recreational area with playgrounds, climbing walls, and a skating ribbon (seasonal). Enjoy outdoor activities and let the kids burn off some energy.

- Evening: Attend a family-friendly theater performance or catch a movie at one of the cinemas in downtown Chicago.

Day 3:

- Morning: Visit the Shedd Aquarium to discover marine life from around the world. Explore exhibits, watch animal presentations, and even touch stingrays in the touch pool.

- Afternoon: Head to the Chicago History Museum to learn about the city's past through interactive exhibits and artifacts.

- Evening: Take a relaxing boat tour on the Chicago River and enjoy the stunning architecture and skyline views.

Day 4:

- Morning: Explore the Field Museum, where kids can see dinosaur fossils, and ancient artifacts, and engage in hands-on exhibits.

- Afternoon: Visit the Peggy Notebaert Nature Museum to learn about the natural history of the Chicago region. Discover exhibits on local wildlife and ecosystems.

- Evening: Enjoy a family dinner at a casual restaurant and relax in one of the city's parks or gardens.

Day 5:

- Morning: Take a bike ride or walk along the Lakefront Trail, a scenic path that stretches along Lake Michigan. Enjoy the beautiful views of the lake and the city skyline.

- Afternoon: Visit the Garfield Park Conservatory, a botanical oasis with lush greenery and exotic plants. Explore the various themed gardens and enjoy the peaceful ambiance.
- Evening: Wrap up your family-friendly adventure with a visit to a local ice cream parlor or dessert spot. Treat the family to some sweet treats and reflect on the memorable experiences in Chicago.

Outdoor Adventure and Nature Exploration (7 Days):

Day 1:

- Morning: Start your outdoor adventure with a bike ride or walk along the Chicago Lakefront Trail. Take in the fresh air and enjoy the scenic views of the lake and the city skyline.
- Afternoon: Visit Grant Park and explore the serene beauty of Buckingham Fountain. Take

a leisurely walk through the park and enjoy the surrounding gardens.

- Evening: Dine at a restaurant with outdoor seating to enjoy an al fresco meal and soak up the vibrant atmosphere of Chicago.

Day 2:

- Morning: Embark on a kayak or canoe adventure on the Chicago River. Paddle along the waterways and enjoy a unique perspective of the city's architecture.

- Afternoon: Explore the 606 Trail, an elevated park and trail system built on a former railroad line. Walk or bike along the trail and enjoy the green spaces and urban artwork.

- Evening: Attend an outdoor concert or performance at one of the city's parks. Check the schedule for free or ticketed events happening during your visit.

Day 3:

- Morning: Venture to the Indiana Dunes National Park, located just outside of Chicago. Spend the day hiking, picnicking, and enjoying the beautiful sandy beaches along Lake Michigan.
- Afternoon: Visit the Garfield Park Conservatory to immerse yourself in nature. Wander through the botanical gardens and take in the beauty of the diverse plant species.
- Evening: Relax and enjoy a picnic dinner in one of Chicago's scenic parks, such as Millennium Park or Lincoln Park.

Day 4:

- Morning: Take a day trip to Starved Rock State Park, located about 90 miles southwest of Chicago. Explore the stunning canyons, waterfalls, and hiking trails in this natural oasis.
- Afternoon: Visit the Lincoln Park Zoo and observe the wide variety of animals. Enjoy

the zoo's beautiful grounds and educational exhibits.

- Evening: Indulge in a sunset cruise on Lake Michigan. Relax onboard and take in the breathtaking views of the Chicago skyline as the sun sets over the water.

Day 5:

- Morning: Explore the Morton Arboretum, a vast outdoor space with an extensive collection of trees and plants. Take a leisurely walk or rent a bike to explore the scenic trails.

- Afternoon: Visit Northerly Island, a peninsula offering nature trails, bird-watching opportunities, and stunning views of the city skyline.

- Evening: Attend an outdoor yoga or fitness class in one of the city's parks. Join a group session and unwind while practicing wellness in the open air.

Day 6:

- Morning: Spend the day at Jackson Park, a green space with beautiful gardens, lagoons, and the famous Osaka Garden. Take a leisurely walk and appreciate the tranquility of the surroundings.
- Afternoon: Visit the Peggy Notebaert Nature Museum and learn about the region's wildlife and natural history. Explore interactive exhibits and discover the diverse ecosystems of the Chicago area.
- Evening: Enjoy a lakeside dinner at a restaurant with outdoor seating. Savor delicious cuisine while taking in the stunning views of Lake Michigan.

Day 7:

- Morning: Take a day trip to the Indiana Dunes State Park and enjoy a day of swimming, sunbathing, and exploring the picturesque dunes along the shore of Lake

Michigan. Take a hike along the trails and marvel at the unique landscape.

- Afternoon: Return to Chicago and visit the Chicago Botanic Garden, a vast garden with beautifully manicured landscapes and themed gardens. Take a stroll and enjoy the colorful blooms and serene ambiance.

- Evening: Wrap up your outdoor adventure with a sunset cruise on the Chicago River. Cruise along the waterways while witnessing the city skyline illuminated by the setting sun.

These suggested itineraries provide a variety of experiences to cater to different interests and timeframes. Feel free to customize them based on your preferences and make the most of your visit to Chicago. Remember to check the opening hours and availability of attractions and activities in advance to plan your days effectively. Enjoy your time exploring the outdoor beauty and nature of Chicago!

Chapter6: Practical Information

Travel Essentials

Visa and Passport Requirements

Most foreign nationals need a visa to enter the United States. A visa may be obtained through a US embassy or consulate. The visa requirements differ based on your nationality. To apply for a visa, you must give the following information:

A valid passport and a visa application form

A recently taken image

Proof of financial assistance

Evidence of links to your native nation

You may also be required to provide supporting documentation, such as a letter from your company or school.

The length of time it takes to process a visa depends on the workload of the US embassy or consulate. A visa application often takes several weeks to complete.

You will be permitted to enter the United States for the period of your visa after you have been granted one. You must have your passport and visa with you at all times when in the United States.

If you are a citizen of a Visa Waiver Program (VWP) nation, you may be eligible to visit the United States without a visa for stays of 90 days or less. To be eligible for the VWP, you must have a valid passport from a participating nation as well as a round-trip ticket to your home country. If you are unsure if you require a visa to visit the United States, contact the nearest US embassy or consulate.

Here are some more Chicago entrance requirements: You must have a passport that is valid for at least six months after your intended departure date from the United States.

If necessary, you must have a valid visa.

You must have a return ticket to your own nation or another country.

You must have sufficient funds to meet your costs in the United States.

You must be able to demonstrate that you have a valid purpose for entering the United States.

If you are unsure if you fit the entrance criteria, you may contact the nearest US embassy or consulate.

Packing List

When traveling to Chicago, it's important to pack appropriately for the season and the activities you plan to engage in. Here is a general packing list to help you prepare for your trip:

Clothing:

- Comfortable walking shoes for exploring the city

- Layered clothing to accommodate changing weather conditions (e.g., t-shirts, long-sleeve shirts, sweaters, jackets)
- Waterproof and windproof outerwear, especially during the colder months
- Hat, gloves, and scarf for winter visits
- Swimwear if you plan to visit beaches or pools during the summer
- Casual attire for dining and entertainment venues
- Formal attire if you plan to attend any upscale events or dining establishments

Electronics and Accessories:

- Smartphone and charger
- Camera or video camera and necessary accessories
- Power adapters if you are traveling from a country with different electrical outlets
- Power bank

- Headphones for entertainment during flights or public transportation

Travel Documents:

- Valid passport
- Visa or ESTA approval (if applicable)
- Travel itinerary and hotel reservations
- Airline tickets or e-tickets
- Driver's license or identification card
- Travel insurance information

Personal Care and Health:

- Prescription medications, along with copies of prescriptions
- Over-the-counter medications (e.g., pain relievers, allergy medication)
- Personal hygiene items (toothbrush, toothpaste, shampoo, etc.)
- Sunscreen and lip balm
- First aid kit
- Hand sanitizer or disinfectant wipes

Miscellaneous:

- Travel lock for securing luggage
- Umbrella or raincoat
- Reusable water bottle
- Snacks for the journey
- Travel-sized laundry detergent (if planning to do laundry during your stay)

Remember to pack according to the weather forecast for your travel dates and consider any specific activities or events you plan to participate in. It's also a good idea to pack a small bag or backpack for day trips or outings within the city. Lastly, be mindful of any baggage restrictions set by your airline to avoid any additional fees or inconveniences.

Phone Communication

When traveling to Chicago, having reliable phone communication is essential for staying connected and navigating the city.

Roaming or International Plans: If you have a mobile phone plan from your home country, check with your service provider to see if they offer international roaming options. This will allow you to use your phone's calling, texting, and data services while abroad. Be aware that international roaming fees can be expensive, so it's important to understand the costs and set a usage limit if necessary.

Local SIM Card: Another option is to purchase a local SIM card upon arrival in Chicago. This will give you a local phone number and access to local calling and data rates. You can buy SIM cards at mobile phone stores, convenience stores, or at the airport. Make sure your phone is unlocked and compatible with the local network before purchasing a SIM card.

Wi-Fi: To save on data usage and costs, take advantage of the many free Wi-Fi hotspots available throughout Chicago. Most hotels, cafes, restaurants, and public spaces offer Wi-Fi access. You can use Wi-Fi to make calls using messaging apps like WhatsApp, Skype, or FaceTime.

Public Phones: If you prefer not to use your mobile phone or don't have access to one, you can find public phones in some areas of Chicago. They typically accept coins, prepaid calling cards, or credit cards for making calls. Public phones are less common than they used to be, so it's advisable to have an alternative means of communication.

Emergency Contacts

When traveling to Chicago, it's important to have access to emergency contacts in case you encounter any unforeseen situations. Here are some essential emergency contacts you should be aware of:

Emergency Services:

Police: Dial 911 for immediate assistance in case of a crime, or emergency, or if you need to report any suspicious activity.

Fire Department: Dial 911 if you need to report a fire or any other emergency related to fire safety.

Medical Emergencies:

Ambulance: Dial 911 if you or someone else requires immediate medical attention or transportation to a hospital.

Poison Control Center: In case of accidental poisoning, you can contact the Poison Control Center at 1-800-222-1222 for advice and assistance.

Consulate or Embassy:

Contact your country's consulate or embassy in Chicago for assistance with any legal or emergency issues related to your nationality. They can guide you on matters such as lost passports, legal troubles, or medical emergencies.

Non-Emergency Police Assistance:

For non-emergency situations, such as reporting a minor crime, noise complaints, or non-life-threatening incidents, you can contact the non-emergency police line specific to the area you are in. Look up the local police department's non-emergency contact number for assistance.

Travel Insurance Provider:

Keep a copy of your travel insurance policy and contact information readily available. In case of medical emergencies, travel disruptions, or lost belongings, you can contact your travel insurance provider for guidance and support.

It's a good idea to store these emergency contact numbers in your phone or write them down and keep them in a safe place during your trip. Additionally, inform a trusted friend or family member of your travel plans and provide them with your contact information in case of emergencies.

Remember that emergency services should only be used in genuine emergencies. For non-urgent matters, it's best to contact the appropriate authorities or service providers for assistance. Stay informed, be prepared, and prioritize your safety while exploring the vibrant city of Chicago.

Money Matters

Currency Exchange Options:

When visiting Chicago, you have several options for currency exchange. Here are the common methods:

Banks: Major banks in Chicago offer currency exchange services. You can visit bank branches to exchange your foreign currency for US dollars. Keep in mind that banks may charge fees or have specific requirements for currency exchange.

Currency Exchange Offices: There are specialized currency exchange offices throughout Chicago.

These establishments usually offer competitive exchange rates and convenient locations. It's advisable to compare rates and fees before conducting the exchange.

Airports and Hotels: Airports and some hotels in Chicago may have currency exchange counters or services available. However, the rates offered at these locations are often less favorable, and fees may be higher than at banks or dedicated currency exchange offices. Consider using these options only for small amounts or emergencies.

Credit Cards and ATMs:
Credit cards and ATMs are widely accepted in Chicago, making it convenient for visitors to access funds.
Credit Cards: Major credit cards, such as Visa, Mastercard, American Express, and Discover, are accepted at most businesses, including hotels,

restaurants, and shops in Chicago. It's recommended to inform your credit card company about your travel plans to ensure smooth usage and avoid any potential issues with international transactions.

ATMs: ATMs are easily accessible throughout Chicago, allowing you to withdraw cash in US dollars. Look for ATMs affiliated with major banks to minimize withdrawal fees. Be aware that your home bank may charge foreign transaction fees or ATM withdrawal fees, so it's advisable to check with your bank before traveling.

Dynamic Currency Conversion (DCC): When using your credit card for transactions, be cautious of DCC offers. DCC allows the merchant to convert the transaction amount to your home currency, but it often comes with unfavorable exchange rates and additional fees. It's generally more cost-effective to decline DCC and pay in US dollars.

Travel Money Cards: Consider obtaining a prepaid travel money card, which allows you to load funds in different currencies. These cards can be convenient and offer competitive exchange rates. However, be aware of any fees associated with these cards, such as reloading fees or ATM withdrawal fees.

It's always a good idea to carry some cash in US dollars for smaller establishments or places that may not accept credit cards. However, avoid carrying excessive amounts of cash and ensure the safety of your money by using secure wallets or money belts.

Before traveling, check with your bank or credit card provider to understand any fees or restrictions related to international transactions. By being prepared and using a combination of cash and cards, you can conveniently manage your finances while in Chicago.

Money Mistakes to Avoid

When it comes to managing your money while in Chicago, it's important to be aware of possible hazards in order to prevent excessive spending or financial problems. Here are some frequent money errors to avoid:

Failure to notify your bank or credit card company: Inform your bank and credit card provider of your travel arrangements before departing for Chicago. Failure to do so may result in your transactions being detected as suspicious, resulting in the blocking of your cards for security reasons. Notify them of your trip dates and places to ensure that your money is available at all times.

Currency Exchange at Unfavorable Rates: Be careful while exchanging currencies. Avoid transferring money at airports or hotels since the costs and exchange rates are sometimes higher.

Instead, go to a respected foreign exchange office or bank in the city and compare rates and fees to obtain the best bargain.

Carrying Excessive Cash: While having some cash on hand for minor transactions or locations that may not take cards is necessary, avoid carrying excessive quantities of cash. It raises the possibility of loss or theft. Use ATMs to withdraw cash as required, and limit withdrawals to a minimum.

Not Keeping Track of Exchange Rates: Keep track of exchange rates between your own currency and the US dollar. Rate fluctuations might have an effect on the value of your money. Consider exchanging bigger sums when interest rates are lower, but bear in mind that it is difficult to anticipate market moves with accuracy.

Scams and Tourist Traps: Be aware of tourist traps that overcharge for products or services. To find reliable venues, do research and read reviews. Be wary of frauds such as overcharging, phony ticket sales, and pickpocketing. Maintain vigilance and rely on reputable sources for activities, attractions, and shopping.

Overspending on Dining and Entertainment: Chicago has a dynamic dining and entertainment scene, but if you're not careful, it's easy to overpay. Make a food, drink, and activity budget and stick to it. To enjoy the range of Chicago's offers without breaking the budget, try a combination of economical and high-end alternatives.

Ignoring Public Transportation: Chicago has a well-developed public transportation system that includes buses and trains. Using public transit instead of cabs or ride-sharing services may help you save money on transportation. To save even more money, consider buying multi-day or unlimited ride passes.

Neglecting Travel Insurance: While not directly connected to money management, travel insurance may give financial protection in the event of unanticipated occurrences such as trip cancellations, medical problems, or lost baggage. Investigate and consider obtaining travel insurance to protect yourself against unforeseen costs.

By avoiding these frequent financial blunders, you may make the most of your vacation to Chicago while avoiding additional financial hardship. Plan ahead of time, be educated, and use sound money management techniques to guarantee a pleasant and rewarding trip.

Conclusion Final Thoughts on Chicago travel

Chicago is a city that truly captivates and enchants travelers from all walks of life. From its stunning skyline and iconic architecture to its vibrant cultural scene and diverse neighborhoods, Chicago offers a wealth of experiences that cater to every taste and interest.

Starting with an introduction to Chicago, we explored its rich history, bustling neighborhoods, and world-renowned attractions. We delved into the city's vibrant food and dining scene, showcasing its diverse culinary offerings and highlighting unique experiences for both luxury and budget travelers. We also explored the city's nightlife, music, and entertainment scene, revealing a dynamic and thriving environment for evening enjoyment.

Moving on, we discussed Chicago's top attractions, including its fascinating museums, captivating parks and gardens, and remarkable art galleries. We provided an overview of major attractions and recommended activities, ensuring that travelers could make the most of their time in the city.

We further discussed transportation options, emphasizing convenience and cost-effectiveness for travelers. Whether it's getting to Chicago from outside the United States or navigating the city itself, we provided detailed information on various transportation modes, including flights, trains, public transportation, and rental cars.

Accommodations in Chicago were thoroughly explored, from luxury hotels to budget-friendly options. We provided tips on finding the best accommodations, ensuring travelers could make informed choices that suited their preferences and budgets.

We didn't forget about practical considerations either. We covered topics such as visa and entry requirements, packing lists, phone communication, emergency contacts, and money management. These essential details helped travelers prepare for their trip and stay connected and safe while in Chicago.

Throughout our journey, we highlighted unique experiences for both luxury and budget travelers, ensuring that everyone could find something special to enjoy in the city. From dining at Michelin-starred restaurants to exploring local markets, from luxury shopping on the Magnificent Mile to hunting for bargains in budget-friendly areas, we showcased the diversity of experiences available in Chicago.

To wrap it all up, we provided suggested itineraries and day trips, giving travelers a blueprint for exploring the city's highlights and venturing beyond its borders. We also shared tips for enjoying Chicago on a budget and finding the best deals on attractions, activities, shopping, and dining.

In conclusion, Chicago is a city that effortlessly blends its rich history with modern attractions and cultural experiences. Whether you're strolling along the vibrant streets of downtown, exploring world-class museums, or indulging in the city's culinary delights, Chicago offers a memorable travel experience for every visitor. With its stunning architecture, lively neighborhoods, and a host of activities, it's a destination that will leave you captivated and longing to return. So pack your bags, embrace the energy of the Windy City, and get ready for an unforgettable adventure in Chicago.

Printed in Great Britain
by Amazon